A QUIET WOMAN'S WAR

A QUIET WOMAN'S WAR
The Story of Elsie Bell

William Etherington

A Quiet Woman's War

First published in 2002 by
Mousehold Press
Victoria Cottage
Constitution Opening
Norwich, NR3 4BD
Re-printed 2006

Cover design by Terence Loan

ISBN 1 874739 24 2

Printed by Barnwells, Aylsham, Norfolk

CONTENTS

Acknowledgements

In addition to those gratefully mentioned in the Foreword, I also owe a great deal to M. Jean and Mme Pascale Maréchal-Ringoet. Mme Elizabeth Liégeois memorably discussed her clear and affectionate memories of her friend 'Polly' (Elsie's code-name in the Comet line) and gave me careful notes on their postwar travels. Professor Martin Dehousse gave me wise advice and shared his first hand knowledge of the meaning of 'Nacht und Nebel', along with welcome hospitality. Mme A. Antoine (line name 'Nadine'), Vice-President of the *Amicale Comète*, has given me very courteous help.

Group Captain W. S. O. Randle, CBE, AFC, DFM, F.R.Ae.S. and Mr Robert Frost have put up with my repeated inquiries in the friendliest possible way, and Mrs Mary Winterton generously shared her late husband's story with me.

The second impression includes corrections and additional information. In particular, Gordon Mellor and Oliver Clutton-Brock have greatly added to my knowledge of what happened to the two Russian airmen after they left the Maréchals.

Advice on shaping this memoir for publication has been entirely the work of Dr Adrian Bell. Errors of fact and interpretation are my own.

W. E.

FOREWORD

It read like an extract from a novel.

'The two airmen were introduced as Americans. The guide left and I gave them dinner. They spoke good American English, but they were not so sympathetic as the other fellows we'd had. E. had to rush to get to HQ in time and B. had left for school, so I was alone in the house. I spoke a little with them and could not help feeling a little suspicious about them. The taller one, in answer to my question, said he came from Jersey City, but he pronounced 'Jersey' with a slight foreign accent. I made up my mind to tell E. to communicate our impressions to the Chief on the very next occasion. Then the doorbell rang. I went directly to ask them to go upstairs to be out of the way in case of visitors, but the taller one was coming to meet me and, grasping my arm with one hand and with a revolver in the other, he said, looking me in the eyes for the first time, "Madame, the game is up."'

In fact it was a passage in a typed seventeen-page item in a file labelled 'Old Students' from my old office at Keswick Hall College of Education, formerly Norwich Training College. Elsie Maréchal, born Elsie Bell, had written it for her parents to tell them what had been happening to her during the Second World War. After her death, in 1969, one of her friends gave a copy to the College (now merged with the University of East Anglia) at which they had trained together as teachers between 1913 and 1915; in all the mass of its records, this was the most unusual.

However did she come to be in this fix, at home, in Brussels, under German occupation? What happened to her after the war? Her friends, by now all dead, had over the years mentioned her in the College magazine and one had written that Elsie was mentioned in Airey Neave's *Saturday at M.I. 9.* In fact he has an entire chapter on Elsie's arrest as a member of the Comet escape line. Clearly, curiosity could not rest there.

Her children, E. (Elsie) and B. (Bob) of her account, were of my generation, and might still be alive. The Belgian Embassy in London put me in touch with Mrs G. Brunsdon-Lenaerts, a former member of the Secret Army, from whose crucial advice came a memorable telephone call from Sergeant 'Gus' Goodwin, RAF, then Assistant to the Defence Attaché of our Brussels Embassy and an enthusiast about Comet, to say, 'I've just been talking to Madame Elsie Maréchal!'

What follows is an attempt to answer my questions, with the generous hospitality and indispensible help of Mme Elsie and Professor Robert Maréchal in letting me see (and explaining) their mother's personal papers, and also showing me her paintings. Still more generous has been their recall of experiences which they have long wished to leave hidden.

They have the school exercise book in which their mother first wrote her story. It begins with this introduction, omitted from her friends' typed copy.

Dear Mother and Father,

Here is a brief outline account of our doings in the war as I promised you. It is not very detailed or descriptive. It is just to fill up the gap in the period of our lives when you had no news from us, from 1940 to 1945. For one thing, the memory of a prisoner becomes as selfish as the rest of himself in captivity and might give a picture rather out of focus, for a little incident such as the gift of a slice of bread is apt to make, sometimes, more impression than the death of a friend. For another thing, it is useless to describe in detail the bad moments of our lives, especially the horrors of the concentration camps. Personally, we desire only to forget it all, so let us, rather, dwell upon the miracle of our escape.

This made it clear that to write only the war story of Elsie and her family, even with the aim of honouring her as an unusual English 'war heroine', would now be wrong. Although the lack of other substantial documents inevitably makes the Second World War the longest part of this account, she would wish it to be seen in perspective. It was like a seismic eruption in an attractive and interesting but quiet landscape, such as that of Norfolk in which she grew up. For her, and most of those who lived through the war, it was a testing and traumatic interruption to life's more important but thankfully less exciting business.

William Etherington

Elsie Bell (1894–1969)

EARLY YEARS

Yarmouth

Elsie Mary was born on 21st June 1894, in Acton, the first of four children of Alice and Robert Bell. Robert managed and later his family lived at a general store at 11 Goodge Street, off the Tottenham Court Road, one of several owned by his adoptive father. Alice came from Great Yarmouth where her father, Henry Cobb Gowen, worked as a carpenter and cabinet maker. Her elder brother, Herbert, was ordained as an Anglican priest in India, and later became the founding Professor of Oriental Studies in Washington, Oregon. His family still remains in touch with hers.

Alice's elder sister, Ann Elisabeth Gowen, became almost a second mother to Elsie, who, as a young child, had a severe attack of rheumatic fever which left her with a slight heart defect for the rest of her life. It seems the family decided that she needed to be in a healthier place than the rather damp shop building in the smoke and fogs of central London, so she went to live at Yarmouth with Aunt Annie. The arrangement continued until Elsie was eighteen. She enjoyed living with her Aunt on Priory Plain, next to the great church – the largest parish church in England, with the town wall on two sides of the churchyard – and although she still kept in close touch with her parents, she and her Aunt developed deep affection for one another.

Ann Gowen was 'Mistress' of the Priory School in Great Yarmouth, which stood on a cramped but picturesque site at the end of the Market Place, its central hall being the thirteenth century refectory of the former Priory. This was a large Church of England Higher Grade School, with nearly 400 boys, 200 girls and 130 junior pupils under a Master, with Miss Gowen as Senior Mistress. It received a higher government grant, had smaller classes and provided a broader curriculum to an older leaving age than elementary schools. The photograph of senior girls, with the Master, Mr Westworth, presiding, Aunt Annie on the left with Elsie at her feet and two other lady teachers in attendance, shows a school with ambitions well beyond the classroom.

At school, Elsie flourished: she learned to love books and developed her outstanding talent in painting and drawing; the family still has a striking animal portrait of a St Bernard dog which she painted in oils when she was only twelve years old. It was not surprising, therefore, that as she moved up the school she chose to follow her Aunt's example and become a teacher.

Girls of the Priory School. Elsie is seated in the front row (extreme left); Ann Gowen is immediately behind her.

For most able girls of the working class and all except those of very well-off middle-class parents who could afford University places, teaching was still – along with nursing – the most likely salaried career in sight. Only those completing the two-year course at Training Colleges were entitled to call themselves 'Trained Teachers'. They monopolised Head Teacherships, and constituted the upper and better-paid half of women teachers in public Elementary Schools; the rest had qualified by external examination or had no formal qualification whatever. By Elsie's time, the half-century-old pupil teachership still existed in name, but had become a form of secondary education with no fees to pay, lasting until at least fifteen, and commonly until seventeen or eighteen. Pupil teachers still had practical experience assisting teachers and starting to prepare and teach lessons, usually in their own schools, but the amount of study time in Pupil Teacher Centres had steadily increased. Some

Centres amounted to senior secondary schools and in fact the boy pupil teachers in Great Yarmouth attended the Grammar School.

Elsie was initially enrolled in the girls' Pupil Teacher Centre, a modest affair, housed in the Education Office but led by a woman graduate. After the summer term of 1909, when Elsie was awarded a well-bound copy of the complete works of Shakespeare as the Centre's prize for Geography, it merged with the existing Great Yarmouth High School for Girls. By the end of her course in 1912 she received two High School prizes, one for gaining First Class Honours at the senior level of the Oxford Local Examination (roughly equivalent to the Advanced Level General Certificate), and the other for being awarded the highest mark in the country in Drawing. We have no evidence of how she spent the next year. The group photograph including Elsie, her younger sister Olive and her brother Stanley is dated 14th August 1912 and may indicate that she had then returned home, but it seems more likely that, with her impressive record, she was employed by the Yarmouth Education Authority as an unqualified teacher gaining more practical experience, until, along with six other Yarmouth girls, she entered Norwich Training College in September 1913.

Olive   Elsie   Mrs Alice Bell
Stanley

College Years

Norwich Teacher Training College had been established 70 years earlier, one of many training colleges founded by the Church of England. Modern eyes would hardly recognise it as a college; it had only 100 students and its three-storey red-brick building, built in 1892 with additions in 1905, looked very like the urban elementary schools of the period. Two grass tennis courts, a croquet lawn and a newly acquired netball court were its only provision for outdoor games; hockey was played in the public park half a mile away.

Students slept in sparsely furnished cubicles; the rising bell rang at six, lights went out at ten; there were two compulsory chapel services daily; and as all cost was kept to the minimum, meals were simple and monotonous, so food treats in parcels from home were eagerly shared. Then as now, society expected teachers' conduct to be irreproachable and as most students were legally under adult age, parents also expected them to be well-guarded. Men visitors, even fathers and brothers, were, of course, forbidden, and unaccompanied outings to the city were allowed only on Saturdays and Sundays from 3 p.m. to 7 p.m., and even then subject to approval after signing-out in advance.

Elsie's children say that she spoke of her two years at the College as the happiest of her life. How could she possibly look with nostalgia on this austere régime? The explanation, perhaps, is that 90 years ago student teachers bore the disciplines with much the same joking tolerance as did nurses under fierce matrons or young men in training for élite regiments. Similar restrictions applied in all colleges and each had its esprit de corps and its Old Students' Club. Students were, after all, glad to be entering a respected career, so they had to be, and be seen to be, respectable. For young women in particular there was enjoyment in simply being part of a lively group, away from homes where, for many, there was much the same control, even less privacy, and, for all, the assumption that daughters were born to household duties.

The full-time staff at Norwich consisted of the Principal, the Revd J.A. Hannah, a bachelor appointed eighteen years previously at the age of 27, and five women lecturers, with a 'Lady Superintendent' as Housekeeper and Matron, and a gardener/handyman. They were supplemented by teachers of the adjoining College Girls' School and some other part-time visitors, including the Drawing teacher, Horace Tuck. The course was intensive and heavily examined by

4

His Majesty's Inspectors; during Elsie's first term, Hannah reported in the *College Letter* (the Old Student Club magazine), 'We certainly were fed up with inspections and examinations throughout the Summer Term.' There had been seven inspections in addition to examinations. The syllabus when Elsie arrived had just been eased so that it no longer required students to study and be examined in the subject matter of every subject taught in elementary schools. Now, it still covered methods of teaching them all, but students needed only to study three or four at their own level – obviously giving no opportunity to reach great depth but at least they had choice. Elsie chose Mathematics, Hygiene and Physical Training and, of course, was one of the two students in her year who chose Drawing (the title indicating its traditional approach of careful observation and representation).

The women lecturers were all experienced graduate teachers and exemplified the generation of late-Victorian career women, as did the part-time non-graduate trained teachers. Hannah not only taught Church History, Doctrine and the Bible, but also the poetry part of the English course, Robert Browning being his great enthusiasm. In her old age, one of Elsie's year-group remembered him as 'a marvellous leader and teacher'.

Although there was little enough time for anything but work, Hannah and his colleagues did their best to offer some relief. With so few students, competitive games could not be played at a very serious level, but, apart from tennis, croquet, hockey and netball, badminton and basketball arrived – not always for a long stay. In both Elsie's summer terms, light-hearted Sports Days were organised, with several members of staff joining in the fun and games. The 1914 Old Student Reunion ended with dancing in the garden, lit by Chinese lanterns and fairy lights; in 1915, the air-raid blackout forced the party indoors. Hannah arranged outings, for instance to the gardens of a large house just outside Norwich and to the folk museum, Strangers' Hall, then still privately owned. In October of Elsie's first year, some students went to a matinée performance of *Peter Pan*, first produced less than ten years previously. In the next February they saw *Twelfth Night*, produced by the great Nugent Monck, a pioneer of the revival of Elizabethan staging, five years before he set up the Norwich Maddermarket Theatre.

Within College walls amateur theatricals performed by both staff and students were a long tradition. Each October, the 'Seniors' (second-year students) presented scenes from Shakespeare, dramatised excerpts from literature and sometimes more light-hearted pieces which they had acted at the closing ceremony of their first year. Elsie's year, in some disgrace, had to admit that their *Twelfth Night* was not ready to perform when their turn came in the summer, but their dramatised extracts from *Nicholas Nickleby* called *The New Teacher* and *Educational Practice* were reported to be 'terribly funny' and Elsie's friends treasured for 50 years her performance as the dull-witted Smike. By the next term, *Twelfth Night* was such a success that the entire programme came to the ears of the staff of a local school, who asked for two special matinées for their pupils.

The Senior year for Elsie and her contemporaries began a month after the outbreak of the First World War, which was to destroy the Victorian and Edwardian world in which they had grown up, and to kill many of their 'young men' and brothers, who rushed to join the colours. The worst slaughter was yet to come, but names of friends on service were soon being posted on the cloister wall leading to the chapel and included in the intercessions at Saturday evening prayers. In January came the first air raids by Zeppelins and the first civilian casualties in Yarmouth, followed by 'Zeppelin Drills' and night black-out of all buildings – a major operation for the College with its lofty windows, for which the Lady Superintendent mustered all hands. By the summer, the *College Letter* said, 'Few of our friends have not been feeling a positive strain', and Miss Teasdel, a Froebel-trained teacher in the College School and part-time lecturer, writing 'A War Scheme for Small Folks', reported that her infant pupils had picked up a whole new vocabulary from the jargon of war reports from the trenches.

The serious faces and long dresses in the year-group photograph taken at the end of their course belie the lives these young women were living when they were released from the long, unsmiling pose the photographer demanded. They knew all about the suffragette movement, the surge of industrial unrest and strikes during their teenage years, and the social conditions in which they were going to teach. The Yarmouth in which Elsie and her six contemporaries had lived was not only a seaside resort but a busy fishing port, with the accompanying noise and drunkenness; many of its schoolchildren grew up crowded into more than a hundred insanitary alleys – the 'Rows'. Students all came to college having worked in schools at a time when a class size of 48 for infants was regarded as an ambitiously small target, and they were entering a profession which had always been in the forefront of social control and improvement. The National Union of Teachers had been formed to defend them against condescending civil servants and often hard-faced school managers.

Hannah dutifully upheld the proprieties but was shrewdly aware of this battleground and what his students thought of it. One of Elsie's year, Constance Oliver, kept until her death a long poem by Hannah, in his own writing, voicing in the style of his beloved Browning's 'Soliloquy of the Spanish Cloister' the Friday afternoon thoughts of a weary young teacher in language which would have earned him dismissal had his clerical overlords seen it. 'Oh yes, Miss Spinks, I will, of course – the nasty spiteful cat; she has her knife in me.' 'Here's a manager ... "Thank you, Sir, good afternoon" – He is a stupid bore; but one must be polite.' He seems to be in tune with the Elsie her more conformist friends remembered; after her death, they quoted as typical her wry remark on teaching practice as she walked into the playground of the intimidatingly named Crook's Place School, 'The iron has entered into my soul!'

Norwich Teacher Training College Leaving Photograph of the 1913–15 group.
Elsie (circled).

As the Seniors' search for work in this far from tranquil scene began, Hannah wrote that Elsie was 'bright and interesting, managing her class well and shewing promise'. She passed her final Teacher's Certificate examination with Credit marks in Teaching, Mathematics, Hygiene and Physical Exercises, and with the predictable Distinction in Drawing which gained her the College Prize. She left also with lifelong friends who admired not only her talents but the vivacity and sense of humour she had brought to their time together. So, having solemnly undertaken to fulfil at least five years' service as teachers, the group dispersed to their first jobs, usually returning to live with their parents. Norfolk, the friends who stayed there and, most of all, Aunt Annie remained part of Elsie's life but she was well enough qualified to compete successfully for work in the most challenging scene for teachers. On 28th July she was notified that she was to be appointed a permanent teacher on the staff of the London County Council.

London

It is a frustration when trying to present a balanced account, that there is little evidence about the first five years of Elsie's adult life, in the career for which she had so thoroughly prepared. She became permanently employed by the London County Council and her salary of £85 per year began at once, but she had then to apply to particular schools from a list advertised in the *LCC Gazette*. It was as well that she was being paid as it took her until 18th October to join the staff of an East End school, Dempsey Street Junior School in Stepney. By the following May the Authority cut one post from the school and Elsie, the last arrival, was told that she must move on, although she could stay for the time being as another teacher was currently attached to a different school. Unsettling as this must have been, she successfully completed her probationary year and was put on the pool of what would now be called supply teachers. There is no further record of where she taught. Four years of supply teaching must have been very testing, but she seems to have served them with some satisfaction and later told her own children of her special delight in teaching in one school with mainly Jewish children, whom she found charming.

The event which changed her life came not in a school, but in a park. An air raid warning sounded, everyone began to run towards shelter and Elsie stumbled. As she later told the story, she was caught in the arms of a Belgian soldier, Georges Maréchal. Georges had been born on 11th December 1892, in a small village near Louvain, the eldest son in a French-speaking Catholic family. After attending a Jesuit school in Louvain, he completed his higher education with a diploma in Horticulture at the National School of Horticulture. In April 1915 he joined the Belgian Army led by King Albert, which held the tiny waterlogged south-west corner of Belgium throughout the war. He had volunteered as an artilleryman and served in the hazardous front-line work of a trench mortar-battery until, in January 1917, he fell ill with pneumonia and a heart condition, and was sent to a Belgian hospital in London. He was a good linguist, fluent not only in Dutch/Flemish and German as many Belgians are, but also in English. The acquaintance, so melodramatically begun, blossomed.

Georges

Early in 1918, with the war still continuing, Elsie and he became engaged despite the slight reservations of both families about foreign spouses. By then, Georges' health had improved, but he was not fit enough to return to the front. He had become sergeant clerk to the Commandant of the Belgian base at Le Havre and, just before the war ended in November 1918, was promoted to the rank of Adjutant (Warrant Officer). He continued to serve in the Le Havre administration until he was finally demobilised as medically unfit in September 1919, and in November was appointed to the staff of the Belgian High Commission in Koblenz, part of the Inter-Allied Rhineland Commision set up under the Treaty of Versailles.

A national event which, because it involved both Norwich and Belgium, must have caught Elsie's attention during 1919 was the return of the body of Edith Cavell, the daughter of a Norfolk clergyman who had been shot for using her nurse-training school in Brussels to shelter escaping British soldiers. She was buried on 15th May beside Norwich Cathedral with great publicity and ceremony. Twenty years later this would resonate profoundly in the lives of the two young lovers.

Elsie's pledged teaching service of five years ended in the following summer and after their marriage on 21st June 1920 in St James' Fitzroy Square, she eagerly crossed the Channel to begin a new life as a Belgian housewife.

MARRIED LIFE

Koblenz

Under the law of her new country, Elsie's married life began with a secular marriage registration in Brussels. For Georges, as a practising Catholic, a third ceremony was needed, but as Elsie was firm in her intention to remain Anglican, he had to obtain a dispensation, having gained the Church's formal acceptance of her ready agreement that any children would be brought up as Catholics. This process proved to be very protracted and, after a short stay in Brussels, the couple went off to set up their home in Koblenz.

The High Commission's duty was to supervise a fifteen-year occupation of the German Rhineland as a security until Germany had paid heavy reparations imposed by the Versailles Treaty for war damage inflicted on the Allies. With several years' experience in the headquarters at Le Havre behind him, Georges held an administrative post in charge of the record and dispatch section of the chancellery.

Elsie and Georges newly married: Koblenz

The informality of the newly weds' photograph together marks them as members of the young generation of the inter-war years. In 1922 Elsie put all her affection and talent into a portrait of Georges which is not only an excellent likeness but uses a newer oil painting style than she had learned at school and college. Elsie was obviously thrilled by her first taste of life abroad, sending her friends snapshots, accounts of rambles by the Rhine, visits to Brussels, and hopes of visiting Vienna. She wrote to her college friends to thank them for their joint wedding present, urging them to visit her in Koblenz, 'a glorious place for a holiday'.

Her third marriage ceremony and registration was in the Catholic church of St Joseph in Koblenz, on 20th February 1922. On 28th June her first daughter was born and named Lilian Grace after Elsie's younger sister who had died at the age of fourteen. Elsie made a charming, tiny pencil-and-wash picture of her sleeping child when she was just three months old – the tints too subtle for accurate reproduction. In the following summer she took Lilian to visit their English relatives and, later, her college friends, many still unmarried and teaching, and provoked a little envy by telling them that she had been holidaying in Paris. Her second daughter, named Elsie (and so, inevitably, 'Little Elsie' for all her young days) was born in June 1924. Then, without warning, a shadow came over these golden years.

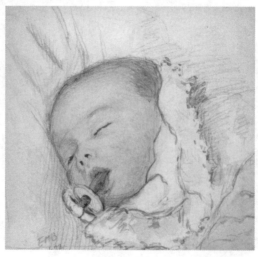

Lilian asleep

On a favourite walk beside the Rhine, Lilian, still a toddler, fell and scrubbed her knee, tetanus set in and after two distressing weeks she died, aged two and a half. Elsie never lost the mental scar; for more than 30 years, through and long after all the family vicissitudes of the second war, she kept Lilian's clothes and toys, never allowing her other children to touch them. Then came another wound when her third child was stillborn.

Robert's birth, in February 1926 was, therefore, a special joy and it is not surprising that he was anxiously cared for when his appetite as a small boy was less hearty than his mother thought it should be. In fact, he and his sister still laugh at their deals under the table when she relieved him of food in return for toys. They recall a secure and happy childhood. Their father had grown up in a family where his father was very dominant, sometimes irascible, and mother's place was with her saucepans – given Belgian tradition of cuisine, a position not without its own honour. Georges was still the final decision-maker, but the home which he and Elsie created gave the children warm love as well as firm discipline, and the adult Little Elsie recalls with a smile how, when she chose, her mother could gently steer her devoted husband's decisions. Both children still speak glowingly of Georges as an example of straightforward honesty and reliability, who hated injustice and unfairness.

As the children grew up, he particularly liked taking them for walks and using his botanical knowledge to interest them in plants and flowers as, no doubt, an opportunity to enjoy in his leisure the original hopes for a career which events had diverted into desk work. Elsie carefully observed the duty of bringing them up as Catholics although she only rarely attended Catholic services herself. The language they grew up with was English and Elsie enjoyed using her teaching skills as they learned nursery rhymes and the beginnings of reading and counting. Books became as important a part of their lives as in those of their parents and showers of them came as Christmas and birthday presents from Elsie's English family and friends, whom they came to know on visits to England.

She had help in the home from Katie, a friendly German woman servant, and so was the more able to enjoy time with the children as well as to entertain friends and paint pictures which Little Elsie and Robert still hang in their homes. She continued to take the children to visit their English family and to meet her friends when this could be arranged; the *College Letter* mentions one such visit in

1927 – perhaps the occasion when she took the photograph of Aunt Annie, now retired, with the children.

Elsie and Bobby visiting Aunt Annie c1927

This materially comfortable early married life was in a Germany aggrieved by defeat, the terms of the Versailles Treaty and Allied armies and military governments in the country west of the Rhine, with bridgeheads on the east bank. The country was also in constant political and economic turmoil. In October 1923, in an attempt, encouraged by the French, to make the Rhineland independent, Koblenz was where one of two aspiring leaders set up his short-lived government. The High Commission staff were in no danger from this; the Belgian and British authorities were firmly neutral, regarding the affair as one for the German government. Georges' fluent German no doubt eased his personal dealings. The Maréchals enjoyed taking their children to visit the farm of Katie's parents and when a colleague married a German, the couple became part of the Commission staff's international social circle.

Georges was always keenly interested in public affairs and was in a good position to follow the politics of the family's situation. Germans of similar social position all around them had their savings and incomes destroyed by inflation so grotesque that a dollar was worth a trillion paper marks by November 1923, when Hitler launched his failed Munich *putsch*. The German Governments evaded paying full reparations which were constantly being debated internationally, so Georges was soon aware that the duration of his job was beginning to look less certain than it had been in 1920. As early as the Autumn of 1926, when she wrote to her College year group secretary, Hilda Pascoe, with proud snapshots of Little Elsie and Bobby, Elsie already mentioned the uncertain future and the mixed feelings she and Georges had about the prospect of leaving Koblenz. She had been only a visitor to Belgium and would have happily stayed in the beautiful Rhineland for many years.

In the event, the blow came suddenly when, in August 1929, an international agreement was made to alter the reparations scheme of the Versailles Treaty and to end the occupation after ten rather than fifteen years. On 14th September Georges was brusquely sent six weeks' notice. His employment would end on 31st October with nothing more than thanks for his efficiency and good wishes for the future. It gave little comfort or practical compensation that he was to learn eight months later that on the recommendation of the Ministry of Foreign Affairs he had been awarded the Chevalier's Cross of the Order of Leopold II for his services.

Apart from the abrupt manner of his dismissal, it could hardly have happened at a worse time. In October the Wall Street Crash led to the great international depression, which hit Belgium, always predominantly a trading and industrial country, particularly hard. Before the year was out, the Maréchals were in Brussels and Georges was one of many educated but unemployed men with families to support.

Brussels

Georges had survived Flanders and virtual exile during the war and a major change of scene was by now nothing new to Elsie. So, still in their thirties, and bonded by the joys and sorrows of their first decade together, they were flexible and robust enough to deal with the move to Brussels, but they would never again enjoy the material comfort of their first nine years together.

Georges had the anxieties and humiliation of a man from a solid middle-class background, who had lost an interesting job and the income that went with it. He could not avoid being aware that his father, a member of the French-speaking Catholic Belgian bureaucracy, secure in his senior post in the Sureté, naturally expected his son to be at least as successful as he had been himself. Although it took him only a month to be back in work, Georges could only find a badly paid clerical post with a petrol company. The first apartment he rented for the family was in Laeken, the North Brussels suburb not far from the great park of the Royal Palace, but a far cry from the charms and riverside walks of Koblenz. Within months, he and Elsie were looking for something better, but it took two years and an interim move before they succeeded.

The children – Little Elsie just five, and Robert three and a half – went to an *école maternelle* where at first language problems gave them more than the usual difficulty of settling in. Robert still remembers being completely at sea; knowing no French and so unable to make head or tail of what was going on, he was teased by other children and followed the teacher round as the only point of comfort in a bewildering and rather frightening scene.

Elsie also had her own problems, although living in regular close contact with the in-laws for the first time was not one of them – they were all very fond of her – but she had her language difficulty to cope with. Georges' indulgence in making English the language of the home had hitherto protected her from needing to add much to her school French. Now it was an everyday necessity. She gradually became fluent and to family and friends her English accent was always one of her charms. Money was short, so there were no more family holidays; visits to England had to be cut; tourism to Paris and Vienna was beyond dreams. The grandeur of Brussels and its parks was only a background to the toils of the urban housewife in the days before detergents, washing machines and other electrical aids – with coal-fired chimneys everywhere making each day a battle for cleanliness and health.

In January 1932 Georges lost his job and, after three months, possibly through his father's contacts, he began a series of temporary civil service appointments in the Ministry of Economic Affairs – ill-paid and below his level of ability. The family removed, no great distance, into a first-floor apartment in Schaerbeek, the large area of north Brussels where Georges' parents lived. It was still not spacious, but had a balcony, and somehow English visitors could be fitted in. That summer, Elsie took the children for a holiday in England, which included a stay in Yarmouth. She wrote about her pleasure at seeing her old College friends again and the children's enjoyment of the beach. By April 1934, Georges was unemployed again and for four months, he worked as a voluntary census recorder before being given more temporary statistical work in the Ministry. At last, in November 1935, he became a permanent Ministry inspector of internal commerce, working in Flanders. This was not by his own choice, and it exemplified an old grievance of Flemish politicians – an official in their region whose first language was French. He had to travel there daily by train, but he always came home keen to ask about what the children had learned at school that day and to make sure they were doing their homework.

Robert was not fired by all the subjects of the curriculum, but he shared his father's fascination with nature, particularly with any live creatures he could find – which sometimes, in normal brotherly style, he put whole or in pieces down Little Elsie's neck. She and Robert remember how determined their father was that they should both grow up to be as hard-working as their mother and he were, and aim to go as far as possible in their education. But both he and Elsie also passed on their pleasures. Elsie always set an example of finding time for books and Georges liked to read out newspaper items and start conversation about them. In winter, Georges played indoor games of all kinds with the children and in good weather he continued to take them for walks and day trips, though he could never again afford longer holidays. Elsie and he loved exchanging visits with friends and family, and they succeeded so well in shielding the children from any sense of deprivation that only much later did they look back and realise what struggles had been hidden from them. The removals did not affect their well-being; this was a family so secure that home did not mean the building in which it happened to live.

In 1936, Elsie was again able to visit her family in England. Missing the children, she sent Georges a comic seaside postcard, declaring, 'Dear Old Man, I'm getting anxious about you all. If there's no news when I get back to London, I'm packing up!' Her English friends continued to come over to visit her in Belgium. In 1937, one of them, 'Win' Jary, still teaching in Yarmouth, reported to friends on her return what 'wonderful little linguists' the children were. By now, the children, apart from being bilingual, were normal little Belgians. Little Elsie never forgot her school's displays of strong national pride on special occasions. 'They played the Brabançonne [the national anthem] and we stood straight and proud, saying nothing and we felt for the country then, you see.' Children also learned the stories of Edith Cavell and Gabrielle Petit – a young Belgian woman also shot by the Germans in 1915 for Intelligence work – and went to lay flowers on their memorials.

This patriotism was particularly strong since the Great War, and it was natural for Georges to share it. After Mass on Sundays, when he took the children to see their grandparents, Little Elsie noticed that his conversation with Grandpère kept returning to their army service under the command of King Albert who had refused to be put under French or British generals and had returned in 1918 with enormous prestige for having kept a foothold in Belgian territory. His standing, cultivated to the point of hero-worship, meant that he personally symbolised national unity, despite the perennial tensions between the Flemish- and French-speaking areas which the Germans had deliberately exacerbated. Added to his constitutional powers, which were greater than those of other royal heads of state at the time, his prestige gave him virtually presidential authority in dealing with the endless series of short-lived governments arising from the fragmented parties elected by a divided society. Consequently his death in a climbing accident on 17th February 1934 was a major calamity for the country. Only a month previously, his influence had encouraged Parliament to resist Flemish separatists' attempts to restore to office ministers of the collaborationist wartime government of Flanders.

Georges took the children to sit on his shoulders in the crowded Rue Royale as the King's funeral cortège passed. The great event had an odd outcome for them. Robert, whose eighth birthday was the day before Albert's accident, boyishly remarked to other children that 'the king had broken his coconut' and this came to the ears of the outraged Sister Headmistress. She demanded to see Georges to question the home influences it revealed. Georges was furious. He promptly moved the children to a secular school, which was of benefit to their education because the work was a year ahead of what they had been doing, and they were bright enough, with their parents' backing, to catch up quickly.

Leopold III came to the throne with great public sympathy, reinforced in 1935 after his beautiful young Swedish wife, Queen Astrid, was killed on holiday when their car crashed, but he could never achieve his father's personal standing. He explicitly set out to act as his father would, insisting on national unity and using his constitutional powers. Georges, as a civil servant and a conservatively minded Catholic Party supporter, was happy when early in 1935, after months of party manoeuvres had failed to produce a government to deal with the economy, the king appointed a professional economist and banker, Van Zeeland, to be Prime Minister. By 1940, during his six years on the throne, the king had had to deal with six different Prime Ministers, the last having four different cabinets. It is not surprising that Georges had animated arguments with his father who, along with many other Europeans, was so irritated by parliamentary democracy's failings that for a time he leaned towards the Fascist solution of strong action offered by Léon Degrelle's Rexist Party.

However, each of them knew, as did every head of family in Europe, that it was not only economic events that threatened the security of his home. Belgium was the country with most to fear from her great neighbour's rearmament after Hitler came to power explicitly rejecting the Versailles settlement. With broad support, Leopold tried to avoid German hostility or subservience to France, whilst strengthening the army, always personally commanded by the king under the Belgian constitution. When Hitler sent his army into the 'demilitarised' Rhineland, with no resistance from France or Britain, bringing gloom to the millions of their people who could not forget the Great War, Leopold decided that the only hope was to declare a foreign policy of 'independence', internationally recognised neutrality having failed his father in 1914. When France and Britain were finally forced into war in 1939, their conduct in the first eight months of 'phoney war' (*drôle de guerre* – comic war – was the French phrase) gave Leopold, as a soldier, no reason to change his mind.

Then came Blitzkrieg, making nonsense of the calculations of the leaders of all three countries and shattering the lives of millions of Continental families like that of Elsie and Georges.

Georges in the countryside

BLITZKRIEG

Elsie's own account of her war from start to finish is the core of what follows.* After her mother's death, her daughter who was fifteen years old when the story begins and so from this point on is referred to as 'Young Elsie', put on paper her own sometimes extensive additions to what her mother had written. Rather than for these to appear as if they were a competing document, she prefers them to be incorporated in the narrative into which we set Elsie's story.

BRUSSELS: May 10th, 1940. 5 a.m.

The booming of guns in the distance awakened us both, Georges and I. Another foreign aeroplane being driven off the territory was the thought that passed thro' our minds and we turned over to sleep again. Sleep, however, was impossible, for the booming became louder and more insistent. At last we were fully awake and aware that something unusual was happening. The anti-aircraft came into action and the crash of bombs added to the noise. We rushed to the balcony and told the children (E. and B.) to dress. A fleet of aeroplanes was flying just overhead, flashing silver in the morning sunshine. 'It's war,' said G. 'Ah, les cochons!' Yes, it was war – a little more than twenty years after the war that was to end wars. Since then all Europe has known war and the Belgians, with their memories still fresh from 1914–18, not the least. So they came out from their homes like the rats of the pied piper in families and dozens, pouring into the routes that lead to France or to the coast, all fleeing from the advancing invader.

On Saturday, May 11th, British and French Troops entered Brussels and were passing all day long with tanks and cannons thro' the principal thoroughfares. 'Thumbs up' was the mutual greeting of the British Tommies and the Brussels population. The same day G. received orders from his office to work in Ypres and Poperinghe on the following Monday. On Sunday evening news came through that the Germans had broken thro' the Albert Canal

---

* Elsie's account is printed here in italics. It is noticeable that she occasionally used some words and expressions that reflected the French which she had been speaking for so long.

– the situation was serious. G. always far-sighted, knew that if he reached Poperinghe on the following Monday, he would not be able to return to Brussels, so it was decided that the children and I should accompany him and stay for a few days in Ypres by E.'s godfather (who had invited us in case of war) until we could see more clearly how the war was turning. Accordingly, I packed up a few things, and Monday morning early we took the train (the last, by the way, to leave Brussels). Arrived in Ypres by our friends we spent the best part of the time listening in to the news. The Germans continued to advance rapidly and on the following Friday, all the people not of Ypres were invited to leave the town. Only one direction was possible – to France – the enemy was drawing nearer. Only one means of advancing was possible for us, as we had no car, so we joined the never-ending stream of refugees on foot.

After a wait of three days at the frontier, where the refugees and vehicles of all descriptions had accumulated to tremendous proportions, at last the frontier was opened, and the whole vast army of refugees poured into France. Everywhere there was a sense of desolation and hopelessness. Even the British troops we passed seemed lost.

About twelve miles into France, they arrived in Hazebrouck where Georges went with Young Elsie to try to buy bread. The *boulangerie* was close to the station and as they came near, the air-raid alarm sounded. Aeroplanes flying very low bombed the station and the whole shop window-pane shattered on their backs, but they were not even scratched. Elsie and Robert, waiting for them to return, had seen and heard the explosions and were very relieved to see them back safely. Then Belgian soldiers began to come out of the station and they were amazed to see that one of them was the children's cousin Paul. Many of them were wounded and he told the family that some of his friends had been amongst those killed in the bombed trains. The troops had orders to stay there and so they had to leave him and go on their own way, carrying their suitcases.

Walking along roads continually bombarded by the Germans overhead, chased from the towns by the English, sleeping in barns or farms at night, we arrived at last on the outskirts of St Omer. A young French officer on a bicycle came rushing from the opposite direction, warning everyone to get out of the way, as there were

German tanks advancing machine-gunning all in their way. So we took shelter in a large farm with over 300 other refugees.

Elsie does not mention being dive-bombed, having to take cover in ditches when machine-gunned, or that, on the way, tired by walking for hours, she fell and sprained her ankle but still had to go on until they were forced to stop at a farm. This was at Blendecques, just outside St Omer, only twenty miles from Calais, where they and many others had hoped to board ferries and escape to England. It was, however, encircled, and even before the German attack began refugees had been refused entry. A mainly British force, ordered to stay and defend it at all costs, held out for five days, suffering heavy casualties until it was overrun and captured. One of the wounded prisoners was Airey Neave who enters the story two years later.

Young Elsie remembered how at first the noise of bombing and gunfire made sleep at the farm impossible, and that the night sky was illuminated by the burning towns. One evening, the farm itself was struck by British bombs. Elsie was with an old servant and a baby in the kitchen preparing supper, when the explosions shook the house and shattered the windows, but, by luck, no one was touched.

We were soon surrounded by the enemy, who came along – the picked troops of the Nazi regime, splendidly equipped and arrogantly proud in the first flush of victory. It was the flower of the German army with hardly the dust of battle on them and with a varnish of politeness that astonished a population having suffered from the brutality of 1914. They spoke English with more ease than French and most of them had English dictionaries in their pockets. On a car was chalked, 'London in sicht' and everywhere, it was 'nach England'. We stayed in the farm about three weeks, always with a faint hope that the Germans might be driven back, but finally we decided to do like the rest and find our way home again. On our way out we had seen the people all leaving their homes and farms, and on our return we found the villages destroyed by bombs and fire, and the poor people returning to their plundered homes. So we returned to our own home, too, but thanks to Georges' family who had remained in Brussels, our home was not plundered.

OCCUPIED BRUSSELS

The Belgian Army's eighteen-day 1940 campaign ended when, after repeated fighting withdrawals to conform with those of the much smaller British and French forces on its flanks, King Leopold, its Commander-in-Chief, decided that a breakthrough of its line was imminent. To prevent a rout which would have resulted in great slaughter, he gave the British Headquarters eleven hours' notice that he would cease fire and surrender on 28th May. He was, unsurprisingly, pessimistic about the Allies' prospects. His Cabinet, already in France, criticised his accompanying decision that honour demanded that he should become a prisoner with his men. Controversy about the King's conduct and his political views began at once and still continues after sixty years. Although fascinating, this is not our subject, but the lives of the Maréchals were directly affected by the peculiar state of affairs which followed when they arrived home.

The King insisted that as a prisoner he could not exercise his constitutional powers. No peace treaty was made and the Germans did not, as in some countries, take over territory (apart from one small district); nor did they set up a military government or inflict a puppet government of collaborators. A military administration under General von Falkenhausen, a traditional soldier unsympathetic to the Nazis, gave such orders as it thought necessary to the Belgian authorities. Before leaving for France, the Cabinet had authorised the civil service and local officials to stay at work, using their usual powers but changing no laws. The outcome was that, although the exiled Government was still at war with Germany, its administration continued to function in many ways. So Georges, after a three-month break, simply went back to work.

As the Maréchals had seen in France, the Germans wished to avoid repeating the damage to their prestige that had been caused by blatantly brutal behaviour towards civilians during the 1914–18 occupation, although the Gestapo did move in with the field forces, overlapping and sometimes competing with the Luftwaffe and Reichswehr security services – the Geheimefeldpolizei (GFP). What Elsie had called their varnish of politeness soon wore thin as acts of defiance and resistance began. Young Elsie remembers the bitterness in Schaerbeek when in neighbouring Evere a German sentry shot a seven-year-old boy for not running off a bridge when ordered to do so.

Only limited material damage had been done during the Eighteen Day war and most businesses, industries and public services had hardly been interrupted. Industrial leaders had little choice about accommodating to Nazi policies concerning the relation of industry to the state; after the weakness of Belgian pre-war governments, some agreed with authoritarian rule and few saw any rational likelihood of a future other than as part of Hitler's New Order in Europe. With the exports and imports which, for centuries, had been essentials of the Belgian economy now limited to this Europe, the German reins tightened and hardship followed.

> ...our home was not plundered. There we took up life again in the normal way, but with lead in our hearts. So severely rationed that it was a serious business to find enough food to live; no pleasure to go to town for the streets were full of the grey-green uniform; German films in the picture houses; no news from the outside world except from German sources; life was decidedly not worth while. The German success was so complete that many people were persuaded that England must capitulate but the Battle of Britain started and to the astonishment of the majority of the population England did not capitulate. Hundreds of invading German bombers never arrived back to their base and, in spite of the constant bombardments, England held out. But we all realised that she was not strong enough to deliver us immediately; we had many days of privation and misery before us. As a general rule, the occupiers were outwardly polite in their dealings with the population, but the slightest sign of resistance was met by severe punishment. The Jews were relentlessly persecuted and gradually disappeared from circulation. Each day brought fresh vexations and stories of German oppression.

This is all Elsie wrote to her parents about day-to-day life under occupation. Long after the war and her death, her daughter found amongst her mother's papers a small English pocket diary for 1936, untouched until early in 1941 when she had started to use it for pencilled jottings about her everyday life. In 1942, perhaps because it was too costly or difficult to buy such things by then, or because she did not wish the family to know about it, she used the same pages a second time, finding enough space for her terse entries, which might only be 'G. Ostend' to record where Georges had been working that day. Either the GFP did not come across it when they arrested the family and occupied the house in 1942 or, if they did, they thought it was only a scrap of family clutter. They certainly failed to realise how much incriminating evidence it contained. We shall use this evidence later but, with the laconic entries interpreted by her daughter, the diary's main value lies in the intimate insight it gives into Elsie's daily concerns and labours as a mother and housewife, and in the authentic detail which adds colour to her generalised short account of 'the normal way' of her family life under German occupation.

* * * * *

Georges and Elsie were as sociable as ever. 'Visit Mme H.' is a recurring entry. These were social calls on Mme Hunez, not enjoyed by Young Elsie and Robert. 'She had no children and when we went there, we couldn't touch anything or speak; we had just to sit still and keep quiet!' M. and Mme Hunez became friends of the Maréchals as a result of a casual conversation between the husbands during one of the long waits on a station platform. Speaking quietly, with Germans nearby, Georges said that his wife was English. M. Hunez, who had a paint business, replied that his wife had worked in London during the First World War. They exchanged addresses and began to exchange visits for conversation in English and sometimes to play bridge. Elsie mentions going at least once with Mme Hunez in order to try to help an English couple, the Dearloves, stranded in Brussels and very hard up.

Notes of exchanged visits with other friends reflect the mixture of normal and abnormal circumstances: 'Have dinner with Mme Moulin. Potato cake. Play whist.' 'Go to Mme Moulin to grind corn.' One visit merited one of Elsie's rare exclamation marks: 'Family T. came. Brought currant bread, jam, sugar with them! Played Pit. Talked politics.'

The arrival of two letters from England was unexpected and worth recording. One dated 4th January 1941, from Georges' sister and her English husband, arrived through the Red Cross in March and replies were sent by the same route. A little later, a letter from a friend in New York arrived and then in May, an uncensored letter somehow arrived from 'Win' Jary in Yarmouth. In August, 1942, Elsie records posting a letter by the Red Cross to another close friend in England, Lilian Seaton, but there is no evidence that it was received.

There are notes of the small milestones which are part of every family's oral history, such as Robert's fifteenth birthday, his coming home with 'flu and Georges' and Elsie's experiment with home brewing, followed by straining and bottling the product. Young Elsie remembered (but the diary omits) the consequent explosions of some of the bottles, which sounded like the start of an air raid. The note in mid-January 1941, 'Burnt last coal. Ate last potatoes. B. breaks window' evoked another memory for Young Elsie: 'With a ball, I remember. Oh, that big window that was broken! That was terrible. Freezing hard!'

The event on 25th August 1942 which Elsie chose to record is that Young Elsie and Robert went together to the cinema; it is, indeed, the only visit to a cinema or other place of entertainment mentioned in the entire diary, no doubt because of the predominantly German programmes of which she complained. Young Elsie remembered the occasion for reasons which the teenage pair could not disclose to their mother; it turned out to be a love story in what was then a very risqué style. The heroine, a woman of the streets, danced in the state nowadays called topless. 'We were stunned. We didn't dare to look at each other. We didn't dare to say a word on the way back and then we agreed that we needn't say anything to Mummy and Daddy; we got all red and flushed!' To a temporary member of the household the day was even more remarkable. His presence Elsie had noted the previous day as 'Melbourne', and the following day as 'Exit Melbourne'. This was in accordance with her usual practice, and 'Melbourne' was Ivan Davies, an Australian crew member of a Halifax bomber, the first evading airman to lodge at 162 Avenue Voltaire. His account of the morning he spent with Young Elsie and Robert we shall come to later.

Throughout the period of the diary, Georges' father was enduring the slow torture of cancer of the throat. At the end of January, 1941, occurs the entry 'Went to fetch stamps for rations of February. New potato cards. Took Père's stamps' (collecting ration stamps to save Mère a journey) and then, 'Père ready to enter clinic'. Shortly afterwards appears 'Père may go to Louvain'. This was for treatment by a Professor who used the harsh radium-needle therapies of the time – twelve needles in the throat for three days, without food. Later, Elsie, Georges and his sister Esther visited his father in Louvain and eventually the diary records 'Père at home. Must eat slops. Can hardly talk.' Constant visits continued and by 19th March, the family celebrated with Père his name day (St Joseph) and 'Had a good meal, egg salad, macaroni.'

By far the most frequent entries are about the grinding toil of keeping the house warm in winter and feeding the family at a time when the Germans, ever since they arrived, had been buying at Black Market prices all the goods, including food, that were unobtainable under the war economy of the Reich. In January 1941, after noting 'Butchers still all shut' and 'Policemen round to order all paper etc. to be taken from attics' (an air-raid precaution against fire), comes, 'Heard German women in tram discussing the stupidity of the Belgians in refusing to believe that it was the fault of England that there was not enough food.' On reading this, Young Elsie added indignantly. 'It was the Germans that were taking it all away! You could see the trains loaded full. All our potatoes, our coal; all that going to Germany, so we had nothing!' The German women were merely echoing their Military Administration's dismally unconvincing 'hearts and minds' propaganda. In by far the biggest city in the most densely populated country in Europe, Bruxellois suffered even more than those in the countryside or smaller towns.

Consequently, it was important to the family that Georges' daily travel into Flanders gave opportunities to add to the larder, even if for him the days were more wearing than ever because railway locomotives and rolling-stock were liable to be commandeered by the Germans. An early entry in 1941 is: 'Trains crowded with people searching for potatoes and food from country. Means of transport likely to be reduced. Trains to be stopped for military purposes.' At the same time: 'G. returned from Poperinghe. Brought back Black Sausage & Pork' – a major achievement. A few days later: 'G. brought nice sardines' from a visit to the coast and later: 'G. Ostend. G. brings tins of meat paste.'

He was taking risks as Black Market dealing was illegal and liable to detection by surprise checks on trains and trams. Nevertheless, as the only means of obtaining something approaching a healthy diet, it was a virtually universal practice. In fact, by early 1941, the German military supply headquarters had copied its own soldiers and units and was buying on the Black Market most of the food needed for its one and a half million men in Belgium, thus driving prices even higher.

The nagging shortage of even the basic filling foods of bread and potatoes pervades the diary. One of the earliest entries is: 'Made chips of swedes. Not nice.' Swedes were normally considered by Belgian standards of cuisine to be fit only for feeding animals. Soon afterwards comes the unusually long entry: 'Made buns with Quaker Oats. No meat. No eggs. No butter or meat fat to be found. Vegetables very dear.' On the day of Georges' return from Ostend with meat paste, the note also says: 'In a queue for meat but no meat. Promise of beef for Sunday ... Made bread with grey flour, Quaker Oats and rice flakes.' The bread sold in shops was universally detested, being a heavy concoction of dark flour and reputed to include sawdust, so the diary repeatedly mentions experiments with home baking when yeast can be bought. A few days later: 'Can't get yeast to make bread so make scones.' Another entry, 'Made pancakes with chestnut flour' refers to an Italian import with which Elsie experimented, making cakes by mixing it with potatoes and a little cocoa or carrots. It was a great day when she could write: 'Flour, 2 kilos beans, 1 loaf. G. brings these from Poperinghe.' Very occasionally a windfall merits an exclamation mark, for instance: '1lb butter!' But it had to last for a month.

An entry in February, 1941, 'Buy eggs at 4 francs 10 centimes each' seems to combine surprise at being able to buy eggs at all with dismay at the high price – about sixpence in sterling values at that time, which would certainly have shocked a British housewife. Interestingly, this is the only reference to prices, although inflation was soaring and Georges' income was unlikely to be keeping pace with it. 'Meat and bones for soup. Obtained beefsteak from butcher!' occurs just before Père's name-day feast. 'G. sows radishes and salad' is the only reminder of Georges' love of gardening, which he had only intermittently been able to enjoy. The same note continues: 'Have potatoes for one day left', and soon afterwards: 'For supper Quaker Oats. No sugar.' In May, 1941, comes: 'Queue nearly 3 hours to have ration books stamped', and within a few days the outcome is: '4 kilos of potatoes for 14 days' – about ten ounces a day for a family of two active adults and two hungry teenagers. For Christmas dinner in 1941, the last they had together, rabbit was served.

The weather during the two winters of 1940/41 and 1941/42 covered by the diary is remembered in both Britain and Belgium as exceptionally severe, with weeks of frost and snow. Homes were heated almost entirely by coal and, in 1941, only half the normal proportion of Belgian coal production was allocated for domestic use. Miners hit their own country by striking for higher food rations to keep them fit to work, and adopting 'go slow' tactics of resistance to Germany's importing some of such coal as they did mine. As deliveries to the house could not be relied on, Elsie had no alternative but to buy coal in ten-kilo sacks from the food and general store, and carry them home, helped sometimes by Young Elsie. Even this supply ran out (hence, 'Burnt last coal' on the day Robert broke the window) and only coal dust could be found. This would not burn in the stove, so the children took on the task of rolling up newspapers into balls, soaking them in the bath and then rubbing them into the black dust; when dried out, the home-made briquettes would burn, after a fashion.

Elsie was clearly keeping the diary only to remind herself of events and details at some future time, rather than to record her feelings or reactions to events, or her inner life. Just once there is a glimpse of her as someone to whom, since childhood, books had been part of life and who is more than just an observer of the war, a diligent housekeeper and a caring mother. In the cold spring of 1941, she uses the diary for notes at some length on a major work – Henri Bergson's *Les Deux Sources de la Morale et de la Réligion*, the book in which he came nearest to orthodox religion. No doubt it had come to general attention because of Bergson's death in January; possibly it was already known that only weeks earlier, very ill, he had insisted on registering as a Jew regardless of being offered exemption. For whatever reason, amidst all her other preoccupations Elsie decided to read and think about it, privately.

We shall come later to the diary's deliberately brief and coded mentions of involvement in the escape line but, without attempting to keep a full chronicle of public events, Elsie now and then records acts of the Germans or of Belgian resistance. Her earliest entry in January, 1941 is: 'V for Victory chalked on walls.' On 17th February, she notes: 'Anniversary of the death of King Albert. Belgians buy no newspapers in sign of manifestation'. In May, she notes: 'Town of Liège ordered to supply electricity to Aix-la-Chapelle. Pylon of transmission blown up with dynamite by Belgian workmen.' She uses the French name, rather than 'Aachen' for the city which, since it was just inside Germany, had been heavily bombed.

On Armistice Day, 1941, she writes: 'Badges of Belgian colours with crepe forbidden to pass in front of tomb of Unknown Soldier. No patriots out on streets between 2 and 4 p.m.' She records the passing effect on her family of Nazi pressure on Belgian Jews: 'Forms from school to fill up certifying the children are not Jews, and giving birthplaces' and on 7th June, 1942 the tightening of the screw: 'Jews obliged to wear star of David.'

Earlier she had indicated the divisions of view between Belgians by noting without comment: 'Professor of Music in Bobby's school preached the good of the National Socialist system.' She omits any mention of the disclosure in December 1941 of the King's secret remarriage to a Flemish commoner whilst still a 'prisoner', which confirmed many patriots' mistrust of him since the surrender. Schools under occupation were as uneasy as the rest of society. Both children found they could detect which teachers were 'patriots', but the knowledge was dangerous. English disappeared from the curriculum and Flemish became compulsory as the Germans tried to court Flemish collaboration. Robert's Flemish teacher was, in fact, a patriot who once, later in the war, signalled his stance by riskily asking his class, during a moment of relaxation, who liked Gershwin's 'Rhapsody in Blue.'

Young Elsie and Robert have memories of schoolmates wearing yellow stars and later disappearing; a friend of Young Elsie was one of the 25,000 Jews successfully hidden by sympathetic Belgians at the risk of their own deportation, but her family was wiped out. Georges came home from work one evening very angry after seeing an elderly lady neighbour thrown into a car after being arrested for sheltering Jews.

'Two young English nurses of Hospital Brugmann sent to Germany' suffices to convey how the event must have brought to Elsie's mind the Edith Cavell story. Once she records: 'German lorry comes to house opposite to fetch back young man lately returned from Germany.' The entry continues: '45 young men taken to camps because of wires being cut in district. Same thing in other parts of Brussels.' In contrast, she also records the strange episode in the air war when RAF aircraft flew in a V formation over Brussels, and the Luftwaffe retorted by forming a swastika.

Among the intentional omissions from the diary were the family's small acts of defiance which began soon after the occupation – Georges' bringing home underground press publications, or the family's regular listening (with many others in occupied Europe) to BBC broadcasts, taking great precautions to avoid detection. Still less could the diary so much as hint that when Georges went to the coast, he was not just acquiring food. From the beginning of 1941, as his work took him into the most crucial areas of the German forces, he used his military knowledge to collect valuable information as a member of *Luc*. This was an intelligence network, already sending couriers to London.

It was the largest of many which sprang up quickly under the second occupation in the lives of middle-aged Belgians, who could use to great effect clandestine skills kept quiet since the first. The exiled Belgian government, which had moved to London late in 1940 when it gave up hope of any deal with Hitler, later boasted that knowing what was happening in Belgium was as easy as looking into a glasshouse. Churchill in his war memoirs paid special tribute to Belgian intelligence which in 1942 had provided 80 per-cent of all agent-gathered intelligence on radar. The theft of a map of all searchlight and night-fighter control stations in Southern Belgium was only one coup among many.

The diary conceals another side of Georges' deep personal commitment to resistance. From early 1942, he was a member of an embryo underground army organised by military men of a conservative outlook to move into action when – if ever – 'H Hour' was declared on the return of Allied forces. It was also to forestall any attempt by left-wing resistance groups to take over. Georges was appointed organiser of recruitment for Schaerbeek, but was never to know how the organisation was to become part of the Secret Army under the direct orders of the government in exile in London. In 1944 its work was co-ordinated with that of the left-wing *Front d'Independance* to play a costly but brilliant part in enabling Montgomery, with just two divisions, and suffering very few casualties, to enter Brussels and Antwerp only thirty-six hours after crossing into Belgium and delayed mainly by welcoming crowds.

To understand the entire family's move into active resistance, which barely enters into the diary, we now turn back to what Elsie wrote after the war.

RESISTANCE

Then we heard stories of English soldiers being hidden by the civilian population, of the poor boys having to hide in woods, and we longed to be able to help them. One day in March, 1941, Elsie came home brimming over with excitement. She had been to her grandparents and had heard her Aunt Esther talking of the case of an English soldier in urgent need of a hiding place. 'Tiens,' said Aunt Esther, 'I suppose your parents would not take him in?' Whereupon, Elsie directly jumped up and sped home to ask our opinion. Well, certainly I needed no persuasion but Daddie, what would he say? When he came home we asked his advice. 'Come along,' he said to me, 'let's go and hear all about it.' So we went, to find on arriving that a place had been found already for the Englishman, but we gave our address in case of need in the future.

Esther kept a jewellery shop in the Boulevard Max, talked readily with her customers and picked up a lot of information there. German notices everywhere in Belgium threatened anyone helping Allied servicemen with the severest penalties. Professor M.R.D. Foot writes, 'As a rule, aircrew and recaptured escapers from prisoner of war camps had nothing worse awaiting them than prison ... This was not the case with civilians who helped them. If detected, they could expect no mercy and received little. They would be tried by a military court; acquittals were unknown. The sentence was invariably deportation to Germany or death at once; a great many of those deported did not come back.'

Georges, very prudent in everything he did, especially since Elsie was English, had already been risking his own life by becoming a member of *Luc*; now he was agreeing to let Elsie and their children run the same lethal risk for the sake of a distant and, by any prudent calculation, unlikely prospect of a free Belgium. Most Belgians saw escapers at this stage of the war as the aftermath of defeat, not future liberators, but, as we have seen, Elsie still believed even after the family had paid and was still paying the price of freedom, that life under Nazi Germany's heel 'was decidedly not worth while'.

She was the first to be involved.

One morning a few weeks later, I received the visit of a priest disguised in civilian clothes. He had received our address and came to see if the accommodation was suitable for the purpose. He was a chief in organising the return of British soldiers through the occupied territories back to their country and also of guiding young Belgians who desired to cross to England to help fight against the common enemy. He was tracked, however by the Gestapo and was forced to flee from his house and hide. He said that if he was not able to return with Englishmen, a young girl would come in his place.

The priest did not give his name and afterwards the Maréchals learned that he had been persuaded to leave Belgium for England in secret.

A few days later the young girl D. arrived giving the password. She explained that lodging was needed for a fellow who claimed the Canadian nationality, but whose papers seemed to prove that he was a Belgian. Could we lodge him whilst enquiries were made? Of course we agreed and in a few hours she returned with him – a poor fellow who had been wandering round Brussels for a week without a home. He had fought in a Canadian brigade of the Polish aviation, had been shot down, taken prisoner by the Germans and trepanned. Inquiries proved him to be a Belgian, and not sound in his mind. He had escaped from a clinic and it was the Belgian police who were searching for him. Our first attempt at patriotic work was not a huge success.

A few weeks elapsed before we received another visit from D. our Colonel – as we called her. She was always so full of energy and enthusiasm. Many a pleasant moment we passed in listening to her spirited accounts of her adventures in conducting the English and young patriots out of the country under the very nose of the Germans. In the beginning they had to cross the frontier line by swimming, or with the aid of motor-car tyres, over the River Somme. When she was not acting as a guide, she was travelling in all corners of Belgium in search of food for the boys, for rationed as we were it was not always easy to feed them.

This time, she said it was not yet an Englishman who needed lodging but two French escaped prisoners from a German camp. One morning, early, G. led them to the station where the guide was waiting to conduct them to France.

D. was 'Dédée', Andrée de Jongh, the twenty-five-year-old younger daughter of a primary school headmaster who lived in Schaerbeek. She was a designer and had also taken a two-year course as a nursing auxiliary during her studies, so when the Germans invaded she worked in a hospital in Bruges. After returning to Brussels in late 1940, with the help of her family, she and Arnold Deppé, a Belgian soldier who had escaped after being captured in the May campaign, set about creating a route out of the country for other soldiers and airmen. The briefcase and school desk of her father, Frédéric De Jongh, became the depot for forged or stolen identity documents produced by his friends. These were essential to enable escapers to pass through numerous check points as she led them into France.

One of the two Frenchmen she brought the Maréchals was Charles Morelle, a tall, fair, handsome man from Valenciennes. The other, Henri Bridier, small and dark, was from the south of France. The guide who met them at the Gare du Midi was Arnold Deppé, who led them safely to France. Nothing more is known of Bridier, but Charles was so impressed by his rescue that he joined the escape line; Valenciennes was in a very useful position just across the French border, which was the first obstacle for parties of evaders on their way south. From September 1941, he and his sister Elvire began to guide groups of evaders from Brussels through France.

A few days after the departure of our two Frenchmen, D. arrived again to ask lodging for another Belgian working for the intelligence service. He arrived at midnight and was to have departed the following day by plane. The next day, however, there was no plane for him. In the meantime (August 1941) D. left with a large party of young men. This time ill-luck followed them. Half the party was arrested and D. had to go into hiding in France.

Deppé had found a safe house near St. Jean de Luz from which Basque smugglers could guide escapers on paths through the Pyrenees into Spain. Dédée, with one British and two Belgian escapers from her part of the group, was guided via this arduous route to San Sebastian, and went on to see the British Consul in Bilbao. He was convinced of the truth of her extraordinary story and contacted agents of the escape section of British Military Intelligence, M.I.9. On her next trip, she made the deal which completed her line, later known to M.I.9 as 'Comet', which was to specialise in collecting and passing out shot-down aircrew who had evaded capture; their skills, based on expensive and lengthy training, made them the most useful escapers back in Britain. M.I.9 set up the crucial last part of the run to Gibraltar, avoiding Franco's police. Dédée was insistent that she would operate as a Belgian civilian, accepting help and advice, but taking no orders from England or the Belgian Intelligence Service in London, and taking money only as loans to defray expenses, for repayment after the war.

Deppé had been arrested in Lille with the other half of Dédée's first party, so never saw his St Jean de Luz link working. Under torture, he gave away no information and survived three of the worst concentration camps, the last being Dachau. Charles Morelle succeeded him as Dédée's right hand man. In the end, as we shall see, he too was arrested; he died of tuberculosis in Dachau ten days after the end of the war.

Elsie gives her version of the line's new development:

However, the R.A.F. was gradually gaining the supremacy in the air and were making terrific raids on the big German towns. Also many of the R.A.F. bombers were shot down over Germany and occupied territory and many brave airmen met their death in flames. There were, however, many others who saved themselves by means of parachutes. They often dropped in fields and managed to escape being arrested with the help of civilians who took them in or directed them to a place of safety. It was like that, finally, a line was organised for these young airmen to pass from one resting place to another, so making the journey in stages to regain their own country. Now D., our 'Colonel', was not a girl to give up working. After the events of 1941 it was too dangerous for her to work in Belgium, but there was plenty to do in France to guide the boys thro' occupied France and to lead them by secret paths thro' the Pyrenees into Spain. Once in Spain it was San Sebastian, a ship and home again.

Despite numerous Gestapo and GFP penetrations, Comet contrived to pass out aircrew until liberation came to Belgium. The last one crossed to Spain two days before D-Day; after that, aircrew were hidden until they could be picked up by the advancing Allied land forces. The GFP were quickly on Dédée's track and made inquiries at her parents' house, but they told a convincing tale of being regretfully long out of touch with an errant daughter. In fact, her father had already taken over her Brussels operation and was carefully recruiting a team to help him.

Then we were left without our 'Colonel' and sadly we missed her visits. The Belgian [hoping to be taken out by plane] stayed in our house, his friends coming from time to time to assure us that soon he would be able to go. Many times he was prepared to start and each time nothing came of it. So the weeks and months slipped by and he decided to leave by another route.

His name was Pierre Courtois, a master at the Athénée de Schaerbeek, Robert's grammar school. He had been trapped by Prosper Desitter (or De Zitter) who became one of the Gestapo's most effective double agents but, through an administrative error, the Gestapo had released him. His optimistic associates' hopes of airlift were unrealistic and they had no access to effective escape lines. Dédée's new specialism in aircrew, unknown to the Maréchals at this point, meant that he was no longer her line's business, so he stayed with the Maréchals for seven months, unable to go out beyond the back garden. He spent his time in study and in helping Young Elsie and Robert with their studies and homework.

Pierre Courtois in the Maréchal's garden

Mme H., a lady of our acquaintance, was occupied in an organisa-
tion for the departures to England. She came and it was arranged
that a member of this organisation should come and talk it over.
Some days after, a man came to the door giving the arranged pass-
word. The journey was discussed and our visitor left saying he would
call again in a few days with the final instructions.

Elsie, writing just after the war, here takes care to follow her rule
of not revealing Georges' intelligence work. 'Mme H' was Mme
Hassé, one of Georges' civil service colleagues, a fellow-member of
Luc to whom he passed on the results of his visits to Flanders. As an
intelligence agent, even though perhaps of one of the many amateur
networks which Belgian patriotism had spawned, Courtois was
more in *Luc's* line of business than Dédée's; M.I.9's advice, the
wisdom of which she and her followers would learn the hard way,
was that it was wiser to try to insulate the different intelligence,
escape and armed resistance networks, in case Gestapo penetration
of one led them to another.

The following day Mme H. arrived to ask if we had had a visit from
her organisation. 'Oh yes,' said I. 'A short dark man with a beret?'
she asked. 'Oh yes,' said I again. 'About 35 years of age, an aquiline
nose, hair brushed back and speaking with a strong Brussels ac-
cent?' 'Just so,' I replied. Then said Mme H. 'It's one of the Gestapo!'
Well, the only thing to do was to find another hiding place for
our young man. Mme H. gave us an address and as soon as it was
dusk we saw him to this address and all trace of his passage was
swiftly removed. For several days we waited in the expectancy of a
visit of the Gestapo. After a few days our traitor called again and
found that the bird had flown. Of course we had a suitable explana-
tion ready. He called once more and then we were left alone. Was it
because he had let his prey slip between his fingers, or that he could
produce no proof against us that he did not denounce us to the
Germans? In any case we deemed it wiser after that to live quietly
and normally.

This agent's name was De Mets, and it was he who had betrayed
Deppé. He had succeeded in deceiving Dédée and Deppé by
ingratiating himself with them through talk (possibly true) of being
involved in distributing a clandestine newspaper. He used the same

method when he called on the Maréchals, and was much more dangerous than Elsie realised when she was writing soon after the war. Later, when he was traced, imprisoned and tried, evidence was given that the Gestapo had paid him a salary of 6,000 francs a month from June 1941 until the end of the war in May 1945.

It was Young Elsie who took Pierre Courtois to his next safe house, that of a lawyer living in the Rue Royale. Later, as a signal of his progress, he sent the Maréchals the sort of innocuous postcard from France which a friend on holiday might normally send, and they passed the news to his brother. After the war, Elsie was visited by a M. Verbanis whom Pierre had met in France, where they had joined forces to make their way through the Pyrenees by their own efforts. Not being linked to M.I.9, they were arrested in Spain and put in the Miranda Camp, General Franco's notoriously harsh internment camp for Allied escapers, where Pierre died of diphtheria. Verbanis gave Pierre's pen to Elsie as a keepsake; she took it to his mother.

Pierre's departure must have eased Elsie's housekeeping problems in the depths of winter when poor people were regularly coming to the door, pleading for bread – always hard to find, even at Black Market prices. Down in the Pyrenees, where the weather was also unusually severe, Dédée had taken Elvire Morelle along with a party of evaders across into Spain, so that Elvire knew enough to take over, if in future the need arose. On the way back through the mountains, Elvire slipped and broke her leg. Using her nursing knowledge, Dédée improvised splints while her tough Basque guide, Florentino Gioicocchea, brought up a donkey and they took Elvire to a doctor who set the fracture. Another Basque guide and his wife hid Elvire until April when she was able to travel and resume work in the line.

By then, the Brussels centre had been badly damaged. In February, when Frédéric de Jongh was in Valenciennes for a couple of days, the GFP had interrogated his wife and elder daughter, Suzanne Wittek (who lived at her parents' home with her children), for a whole day at their headquarters. On his return he had hurriedly gone into hiding, leaving school and home. This was at the time when the Maréchals were trying to get Pierre away and, after school one day, Young Elsie was sent by her mother to the De Jongh's home, less than three-quarters of a mile away in the Avenue Verhaeren, to see whether they could help. Mme De Jongh and her sister-in-law

Eugénie, who lived with her, were very worried and warned Young Elsie not to call again as their house was probably under GFP surveillance.

For several weeks, Frédéric de Jongh continued leading the Brussels operation from a hiding place with the help of his team, but with the GFP putting a price of a million francs on his head, he left Brussels at the end of April and joined the line's Paris staging centre.

After Young Elsie had been warned off, Eugénie (Aunt Ninie) called on Elsie, whose pocket diary entries at this time began to include frequent entries of 'La Tante'. She arranged a new route for correspondence for Dédée's family which had been coming to the Maréchals' as a safe letter box and which Young Elsie, as a very young-looking schoolgirl, had previously been able to take safely to the De Jonghs. The mail would be addressed to Nelly Deceunynck, a school friend of Dédée, who lived with her parents at the corner shop they ran. Aunt Ninie could join their stream of customers and pick it up without detection.

On 8th May, the GFP arrested several of De Jongh's team, including Charles Morelle, who was paying one of his many visits to Brussels. After De Jongh's departure to Paris, his work had been taken over by Henri Michelli, a very active member in several resistance activities. What he did not know was that the Gestapo had already penetrated more than one of them, and also knew a good deal about Comet. He was incautiously giving a dinner party to three parachuted intelligence agents, as well as Charles, when the Gestapo decided to pounce; they later claimed to have made 225 arrests as a result of this *coup*. The entire Brussels collecting centre was temporarily out of action just as the good weather was assisting the RAF bombing campaign to build up; more aircraft were being brought down and more evading aircrew were needing to be returned to Britain.

Control of the line's work was quickly restored, however, by another of De Jongh's team, Baron Jean Greindl. He had become director of a Swedish feeding centre set up in the Rue Ducale for the poorest children in Brussels, under the eye of a wealthy Swedish woman, Mme Scherling, who was on good terms with General von Falkenhausen. Thus placed above suspicion in more senses than one, he reinforced the team with acquaintances from his own social milieu and other carefully chosen recruits.

The Maréchals had stayed low during this period and thought that they were out of danger. Their house was well situated, in a broad street, not overlooked at the front or back. In her diary, Elsie notes one visitor who used this advantage, Elvire Morelle, who was not under any suspicion. She came openly for a normal permitted family prison visit early in June to see her brother Charles in the St Gilles Prison, no doubt having long since heard from him and Dédée about the Maréchals. She came for another overnight stay on 25th June with Rénée, Charles' wife, to visit him again.

Although she was thrilled by the clandestine activities going on around her, Young Elsie was reaching a peak in the normal life of someone approaching her eighteenth birthday. She was absorbed with her school-leaving examinations which ended in July and was soon going to take the admission examination for entry to the Institut Edith Cavell, to train as a nurse. Her mother told how these plans changed.

Then one day we were asked if E. would like to help at the headquarters of the organisation during her holidays. She didn't need to be asked twice. At last her dreams were coming true and she was going to work for the English. So when her final exam. was successfully passed, she embarked on a work of absorbing interest. There were travelling bags, combs, toothbrushes, soap etc. to buy for the journey of the R.A.F. boys, food to fetch and distribute for them, suitable clothes and shoes to find, for they mostly arrived in old clothes that the country people had given them to replace their battle dress. There was even the important task of going into the country to fetch airmen who were signalled as having fallen in an odd place and also of conducting them to town to be photographed for their passports and to and from their lodging houses to the station.

This version of another turning point in the life of the family does not, of course, mention that it was one of the times when Georges was swayed by his wife's persuasion. The suggestion arose during a visit by Suzanne Wittek. Always concerned for the children's education, Georges agreed that Young Elsie could work for Greindl during her summer holiday until she started her nursing course in late September.

On 2nd July, before Young Elsie had even started work with Greindl, Suzanne was arrested again, having been involved in a

41

scheme to bribe Michelli out of prison, and this time she herself was kept in St Gilles Prison.

Four Months in 1942

Young Elsie took her last examination on 13th July (and was later to hear that she had passed with high marks), and at once went to see Baron Greindl in his office in the Rue Ducale. She was struck by the faded grandeur of the long panelled room with its tall windows, ancient furniture, and worn carpets and curtains. Suzanne Wittek, who had helped him to take over after her father left, had recommended her and, as the Maréchals had been trusted if unobtrusive members of the line since its foundation, Greindl accepted her without hesitation. The tiring but otherwise unexacting job of shopping for evaders' travel goods, which inevitably often meant competing with the German forces canteens on the Black Market in what one of its own economists was to call a 'country of smugglers of both sexes', offered him the opportunity to assess her. He gave her the cover of working in the basement feeding centre – known in Brussels as the Swedish Canteen – where each day, poor children were given a spoonful of cod liver oil and served a warm meal. Greindl, a devout Catholic, was an outstandingly caring plantation owner in the Belgian Congo, trapped by the war on a visit with his wife and young child, and had taken on the Canteen as a social obligation. He was helped in the security and management of the Canteen by an efficient and discreet retired officer, Commandant Bidoul. Young Elsie found Greindl very considerate and thoughtful in his dealings with everyone who worked with him.

She quietly watched and listened to Greindl's friends and helpers coming in and out on the line's business. She was particularly intrigued by those with the refinement and style of an upper class she had never previously encountered, although as everyone in the line had a code name, she only afterwards learned the real names – and often titles of nobility – of most of them. She also enjoyed the mixture of amusement and danger in the rush to hide compromising papers, parcels and false identity cards if Madame Scherling swept in on one of her lady bountiful calls to see that the Canteen was running to her satisfaction. She used to call on her way to or from riding, always in full habit with whip and riding boots and the staff knew they would have trouble keeping her happy. One day, she brought General von Falkenhausen to be introduced to Baron Greindl, who must have greatly enjoyed the situation.

Baron Jean Greindl

*Young Elsie at work
during the war*

Greindl asked Young Elsie to suggest a code name for herself, but did not greet her proposal of 'Mickey' with enthusiasm and after one or two other attempts, she reverted to being Little Elsie. (Her mother became 'Polly' and that name stuck through all her later experiences.) Greindl's own witty code name was 'Nemo', Latin for 'Nobody' and the name of the submarine captain in Jules Verne's *80,000 Leagues under the Sea*.

He soon saw in her the kind of girl Dédée liked to use – intelligent, committed and looking so much younger than her real age that she could move about unnoticed by the German security services. She also had the rare qualification of being perfectly bilingual in French and English. He must have judged her to be uncommonly mature to have decided to send her, so soon after her eighteenth birthday, to outlying villages for what would nowadays be termed 'cold calling' on the priest or schoolmaster. Her purpose was to win their confidence and finally tell them how to contact the line if any Allied aircrew came down in their district.

Peggy Van Lier, one of the ablest of Greindl's team, trained her in this and her other new, demanding duties; they always spoke French together, although Peggy, having grown up in South Africa, was also bilingual in English.

In later life, Young Elsie, with understatement surely learned from her mother, recalled, 'It was always a bit difficult, because I would arrive and the man didn't know me at all. He didn't know if I was from the German side. If you talked about a bit of everything and could sense what side he was on, you could say, "If ever you hear there's an aircraft come down in your area and there is anyone looking for somewhere to be hidden, this is where you should write to." Later, I went to look for men who had come down in places quite far away and were hidden in barns or woods, and bring them to Brussels, to different secure hiding places on Baron Greindl's list. Then I went into town with them to have photos taken that would be used for their false papers – identity cards, Ausweise (passes) – needed to pass the line of demarcation in France. In the Rue Ducale, they had loads of them hidden – identity cards and the like; they had to steal the right stamps from the different offices and each man had to have a false name and all sorts of details. That was Baron Greindl's business and he was very skilful at it. At the indic-ated day, I would take them to the station where guides for the journey waited. My English was a help, but out of the house the word was given that silence had to prevail so that they wouldn't give themselves away. I worked with the very active Peggy on this and was very happy about it. Then came the day [24th August] Mother wrote about, when I brought Ivan Davies home. As I was working actively in the line, it would have been best not to have anyone lodging in our house, but because of the number of airmen, necessity made the rules.'

One dinner time, she arrived beaming with satisfaction. 'Ma,' she said, 'I've got one for us. He's in the sitting room!' Directly, I understood and going to the sitting room I found a splendid fellow there – an Australian. It was in August, the period of many big raids. Many planes were shot down; consequently there was a shortage of lodging for the parachutists, so we had the honour and pleasure of lodging the boys too. Then followed a very busy period. When our Australian was safely gone, there was a Canadian, then several Englishmen and even a Pole and an American. How happy we were to, at last, have some real English boys with us.

Elsie's 'we' fails to conceal her delight in striking her own blow for freedom by giving an affectionate welcome to the 'boys', not in fact all English, most only a few years older than Young Elsie, who recalls, 'She loved it. She was a mother to them. They were all such nice men, young, in excellent physical condition. They brought us health and a whiff of victory and the certainty of victory to our side. We had the feeling of being useful, and inside the house we could forget German oppression.'

Flying Officer Ivan Davies had been navigator of a Halifax shot down over Duisburg on 4th August. Alone, he made his way across the Albert Canal into Belgium and was picked up by the line. In his book *Rescued by Comet* is an account worth retelling of the shopping trip during the morning before Young Elsie and Robert's memorable cinema visit, mentioned earlier. Young Elsie (whose age he guessed wrongly) and Robert took Ivan and another airman by tram into the city centre to buy razors, shaving soap, toothbrushes and toothpaste. By now all RAF aircrew carried two photographs for false papers as part of their escape kit, but sometimes they were unsuitable, or more were needed, as on this occasion. They went into two department stores which had automatic photograph booths, but they were not working because of electricity cuts. In a third, the photographs were taken and whilst they were being developed, all four had an ersatz ice-cream. When the pictures arrived, Elsie passed them round.

She remarked on the good likeness and we strolled casually from the store, Elsie fingering materials on the way. The aplomb of this 15 year-old girl gave me confidence. Until then I had been on the alert for errors she might make due to youth and inexperience but I now felt that her intelligence and good sense made her aware of the times when it paid off to take a calculated risk.

A short time after Ivan Davies went away, Earl Price, a shy Canadian of about Young Elsie's own age, was one of those she had to collect. She took a train to the station for Averbode, about 30 miles north-east of Brussels, and walked nearly six miles to the village of Blauwberg where Price, after hiding in a wood, had been brought to a small boarding house. All went well – train, tram and home to Elsie whose diary says, 'Evening Canterbury', the name of his home town in northern Ontario. About thirty minutes after their departure the GFP arrived in Blauwberg and arrested the boarding house keeper, Mme Delogie.

Price stayed a few days before a group of ten men was formed to go to France. The diary says, 'September 4th Exit Canterbury'. The diary also says 'Institute Edith Cavell' because that was the day of Young Elsie's entrance examination. When she heard that she had passed, Georges paid her registration fee and wanted her to enter the course at the end of the month. However, Greindl was finding her so useful that he asked whether she could carry on her full-time work for him and, once more, Georges accepted her mother's gentle pressure to the extent of the compromise that she should postpone her entry until the Spring 1943 intake.

Greindl was a gifted amateur, having picked up what he knew of the evasion trade from Dédée and her father, also self-taught. By now M.I.9 was feeding in its professional ideas but Greindl had to be inventive in response to how events on the ground unfolded. More and more airmen were being collected, particularly in the Namur area. Collecting them wasted the time and growing skills of Elsie and others in his team, and could not keep pace with the flow of evaders, so Greindl devised a new plan. Guides from Namur would bring small groups of airmen to Brussels. Notice of their arrival would be sent several days in advance by plain postcards, addressed to the shop of Nelly Deceunynck's parents, saying 'Packet (*colis*) to collect at the usual place at ... o'clock on ...' Nelly would bring the cards to Young Elsie at home and, in case her long hours of office work prevented this, Young Elsie would call regularly in the shop to see if there was a card to pick up.

'The usual place' was St Joseph's church in the Square Orban, not far from the Luxembourg station at which the trains from Namur arrived. The guide was to go there with his *colis* near the confessional of Fr Costenoble who was such a popular priest that there were always people waiting and moving in and out of the church.

St Joseph's church in the Square Orban

The guide and Young Elsie would learn to recognise one another, although they did not know each other's name. She was to ask the guide quietly, 'What's the time?' The reply had to be, 'Always the same.' Then she would go outside to one of the seats in the park in the square and after a few minutes the guide and his *colis* would follow her. She would ask the *colis* one by one, out of the hearing of the others, security questions to which she knew acceptable answers: name, rank, service number, the place and date where they came down, the type of aeroplane, the number of men on board, their functions, what happened to the other men on board, and some less obvious, such as a secret number on the radio equipment and the name of a periodical of the Royal Aero Club which was always in the RAF aircrew messes. These had been sent by M.I.9 to Dédée early in the summer after another line had detected infiltration by German agents pretending to be RAF men, and were revised from time to time. If satisfied, Young Elsie would take the airmen either home or to another safe house. If not, she would ask them to wait and report back to Greindl. It was an elaborate procedure but it worked well.

Elsie's list of house guests during this period, with dates where they can be found in her diary is:

Ivan Davies (Melbourne) 24th–26th August
Earl Price (Canterbury) Left 4th September
Anton Wosiack (Warsaw) 7th–9th September
Ralph Van den Bock (Guildford) 7th–9th September
Jack Cope (Norbury) Arrived 9th September
Ted Bradshaw (Boston) Arrived 9th September
Robert Brown (Yorkshire) For a meal only on 11th September
Jack Winterton/Winterbottom (Wembley) For a meal only on
11th September
Darryl Mounts (North Dakota) Arrived 22nd September
Bill Randle (Devon) Arrived 23rd September
Lorn Kropf (Ontario) 4th–6th October
Aleksii Stadnik (Kiev)
Piotre Penchuk (Vladivostok)
Jack Griffiths For a meal only, probably on 11th November

All reached England, each with his own evasion story.

Bob Brown, the wireless operator and Jack Winterton, the bomb-aimer, jumped from the same Halifax and landed in the same field where, as they had been taught, they buried their parachutes. They lay there, watching the torches of Germans combing the surrounding woods until they gave up and went away without thinking of looking in the open field. When day came, Bob and Jack walked along a lane until they met a Belgian who took them to a farm. There they were hidden, eating in the barn by day and sleeping in the house by night until the line collected them and took them to Namur. They were the first and last evaders to be helped by the farmer, M. Delbruyère and his wife, who were traced and arrested. When Young Elsie took them home, the house was already full, but Elsie welcomed them and gave them a meal (which must have seriously reduced her larder). Young Elsie took them to another larger safe house, that of Mme Elizabeth Warnon and her friend Elizabeth Liègeois (line name 'Constance'). Their numerous airmen lodgers referred to them as 'the two Betties'. In 1950, they visited Jack and his wife, who remained lifelong friends with them and with the Browns.

Sergeant-Pilot Bill Randle's Wellington bomber had been carrying as a supernumerary Darryl Mounts (an officer of the recently arrived American Air Force) for experience. Bob Frost, the rear gunner, also managed to avoid capture and walked westwards. Not realising that he was in Belgium, he attracted suspicion that he was a Gestapo infiltrator by speaking good German, which he had learned in Germany before the war. Still not feeling he was trusted, he believed 'the Betties' tested him by showing him Mounts's identity photograph. Bob had only met the American shortly before take-off but recognised him. After a relieved reunion with Bill and Darryl, he was moved to another safe house before meeting the others and a Polish airman, Teddy Frankowski, at the Maréchals' to go to the Gare du Midi for the journey home.

Elsie wrote a calm account of her most difficult guests.

In October we had two Russians. They spoke only Russian, so we found an interpreter. They claimed to be Ukrainians of the Soviet Air Force brought down over Germany, taken prisoner, and to have escaped from the camp and to have crossed Germany on foot to Belgium. Our speciality was to pass fellows of the RAF, but still we passed these Russian boys on to Paris, too.

They had arrived famished and at table ate everything in sight without using knives and forks. After they left, she found that they had raided the larder and emptied jam pots, leaving the empties hidden in the W.C. When given new clothes, they put them on over their old ones. These primitive survival techniques had no doubt enabled them to arrive at 162 Avenue Voltaire and would have surprised the two Elsies less had they encountered them three years later.

They worried Greindl even more because the Germans were constantly trying to infiltrate the Line. Unknown to the Maréchals, only five days after they welcomed Ivan Davies, another very active family, the Dumons, had been arrested*. Now this strange pair had been collected by the Namur centre and when they arrived at St. Joseph's, Young Elsie had been unable to use the normal set of test questions. She reported back to Greindl and he went to assess them for himself. He decided to risk sending them to the Maréchal's for the night and sent a Polish speaker to see them. He was sufficiently satisfied to let them stay and be passed on, using one of his most trusted helpers, the Comte Georges d'Oultrement, to escort them to Paris. Gordon Mellor, a Halifax navigator and another RAF man, Michael Joyce, also being led by another Comète courier, noticed the two distinctly odd-looking men on another platform of the Lille station on 17th October. Two days later, Stadnik joined them, with three others, for the train journey to Bayonne and on the night of 21st/22nd October, Mellor, Joyce, Lorn Kopf and Standik were led to San Sebastian by Dédée and Florentino. After the standard journey to the Madrid Embassy, they finally reached Gibraltar with a large group on 26th October. Stadnik was at once separated for special attention, flown to England on the following day and interrogated by M.I. 9 on 31st October. Penchuk clearly interested M.I. 9 less and arrived at Gourock by sea on 20th November, for interrogation the following day. Whether they eventually reached Russia is not clear.

The Maréchals were too valuable to continue risking them as a safe house, so apart from giving Jack Griffiths a meal before going to the 'Two Betties', the Russians were their last lodgers.

---

* The father was a member of Luc and the younger daughter, Andrée, worked in both Luc and as 'Nadine' for Comète. The elder daughter was living in the hospital where she worked, so escaped arrest and as 'Michou' was to become a key member of Comète, rebuilding and leading it after devastating arrests in early 1944.

It seems likely that it was now, when she could no longer look forward to having any more young airmen to stay, that Elsie found a space in her old diary to write her guest list, including their home towns. She never foresaw that her house might at some time be searched by the GFP. She also kept (and the Germans never found) these three written messages from her guests which came back along the line from Spain.

My brave Belgian friends,
Thanks to your kind and courageous assistance I am now in a place of safety. If ever you are in my country, please write to me and give me the opportunity to repay you in part for all you have done for me.

Yours sincerely,
Ivan H. Davies

My dear friends,
Here I am in S.S. I arrived in S.S. o.k. so it's fine and I want to thank you once more. It was so kind of you to help me. I am sure that with out you I be not able to continue my journey. I hope that I see you I mean all of you after the war in much better and happier time so for now cher-i-o

Your most sincere Polish friend,
Tony

San Sebastian,
24/9/1942

Dear Friends,
As you can see from the address, I am now safely arrived in Spain. We had a good 'voyage' across the mountains despite some heavy rain. We leave here today for the last but one leg of our journey home. I should like to take this opportunity of expressing to you my eternal thanks for all you have done for me and my friends at such incredible risk to yourselves. I hope that when this wretched war is over, we shall be able to meet again and talk 'freely'. Well, here's to victory and bless you all.

Yours very gratefully,
Ralph Van den Bock
Flight Lieutenant, R.A.F.

After the war, Ivan Davies told Elsie that he arrived back at his squadron to find that in the three months he had been away, it had been wiped out, twice. He hoped to be posted to another operational squadron or allowed to transfer to the Royal Australian Air Force but was angry and disappointed to be kept by the RAF and posted to training duties in England on the grounds that he knew too much about the escape route to risk capture and interrogation. Ralph Van den Bock was also in touch with Elsie after the war and told her that he was back in England only five weeks after being shot down. He was an air gunner but succeeded in being accepted to train as a pilot and by the time he was qualified the aircrew casualty rate had become so high that he was allowed to return to operations. He was then fortunate enough to survive two tours of twenty-five bombing flights.

*   *   *   *   *

In Brussels in the autumn of 1942, with Young Elsie due to become a student again in another few weeks and Robert still a schoolboy for nearly three more years, it seemed that Elsie's personal part in the battle for freedom would now be no more exciting than keeping the family fed and occasionally giving Elvire Morelle bed and breakfast.

18th NOVEMBER 1942

The lull lasted just over a fortnight. In her usual succinct style, Elsie told her parents what happened next.

On November 18th, 1942, E. was due at headquarters at 2 p.m. Just as we were sitting down to table at mid-day B. went to answer a ring at the door. There were two fellows with a guide whom we knew from Namur. The two airmen were introduced as Americans. The guide left and we gave them dinner. They spoke good American English, but they were not so sympathetic as the other fellows we'd had, E. had to rush to get to H.Q. in time and B. had left for school, so I was alone in the house.

I spoke a little with them and could not help feeling a little suspicious about them. The taller one in answer to my question said he came from Jersey City, but 'Jersey' he pronounced with a slight foreign accent. I made up my mind to communicate our impressions to the chief on the very next occasion. Then the doorbell rang. I went directly to ask them to be upstairs to be out of the way in case of visitors, but the taller one was coming to meet me, and grasping my arm with one hand and with a revolver in the other he said, looking me in the eyes for the first time, 'Madame, the game is up.' The other small fellow had opened the door and let in another man of the G.F.P. (Geheime Feld Polizei). So I was forced into a chair, and the three of them sat around, revolvers in hand, making me speeches on the seriousness of the case and recommending me to speak out all the truth. We were all going to be decapitated they said and in the meantime I was going into jail to reflect. I was allowed to touch nothing and was obliged to accompany the first comer to the corner of the street where a car of the G.F.P. was waiting for us.

The two so-called American airmen were Germans in disguise. They'd succeeded in entering the line at its source and had followed it up to Brussels. Sad to say, one who had worked in our line had turned traitor, and so made such a thing possible. Then followed arrest after arrest in Namur, Ciney, Brussels etc.

When E. returned home she found eight G.F.P. men awaiting her. They forbade her to go into the kitchen saying that her mother was shot down there, and that her turn was coming. B. on arriving home from school and G. on arriving home in the evening were each in their turn arrested and taken to prison.

This was the first account of the events of that day to be put on paper, but it has never been published. After his celebrated escape from Colditz, Airey Neave was, in May 1942, appointed as junior member of I.S.9(d), a two-man section of the British escape and evasion organisation, M.I.9. In *Little Cyclone*, published in 1954 and still the only biography in English of Dédée de Jongh, Neave gave his first version of the day. His more substantial *Saturday at M.I.9*, published in 1969, also tells the story in a chapter entitled 'The Maréchal Affair'. This, which he says was what Elsie ('an attractive Englishwoman') told him when they met after the war, differs in details from his earlier version but is so similar that both were almost certainly based on the same interview. Both accounts, in his vivid style, include dialogue and oddly give the date as 19th November. It is not surprising that his great personal qualities and skill as a writer have led all later writers about the line to use what he wrote as the authority for the day's events and to give it the same date. However, although she was at the centre of this disastrous day for the line, no one has ever asked the younger Elsie for her full version of what happened, which is still engraved indelibly in her mind and set down on paper in French not long after her mother's death. Whilst not differing factually from what her mother had written and which it vividly supplements, it differs on some points from all others and so should be told in full, inseparable as it was from all that she and her mother were about to endure.

She came home from the Canteen at about half past eleven, having found no one there to give her any duties. A letter in an envelope of a common commercial type, made of green paper, came through the letterbox, hours after the normal time for post to arrive. Earlier line correspondence had sometimes come in such an envelope, so she put it in her bag to take when she went back to the Canteen after dinner, but then wondered what it really was and opened it, to find only a small piece of paper announcing the arrival of two *colis* at 11.30 This was very disturbing. Not only was it now impossible for her to get to St Joseph's in time, but the rule was that notice of delivery of *colis* was sent on postcards, never in an envelope, never to the house and always two or three days in advance. The

54

Elsies had no sooner started to discuss the problem when the door bell rang and there was Nelly with a guide from Namur and two men in civilian clothes. The guide said he had waited at St Joseph's for some time and as Elsie did not arrive took his *colis* to the only Brussels line address he knew, the Deceunynck's corner shop to which the postcards were sent, where Nelly happened to be at home. The line's security was so well compartmentalised that the only line address Nelly knew was that of the Maréchals, so she had brought the three there. All Elsie could do was to ask the two men in as she had always done with evaders and Nelly and the guide then left. Robert had come in from school and dinner was ready so she laid two more places and invited the men to the table. Young Elsie decided to ask them the usual questions during the meal, to avoid delaying its being served.

Airmen usually relaxed and enjoyed talking as soon as they were welcomed in English. From the start, these two seemed not to want to talk and were shut in – not at all *sympathique*. They said they were American and the shorter of the two who did most of such talking as went on spoke good English. They looked pale and did not want to eat much, saying they had drunk too much whisky on the previous day. Trying to relax them, Elsie said that she had previously had an Australian and a Canadian to stay. Young Elsie then said that they had a routine, and she was going to ask them some questions, remarking that they didn't look like Americans. The shorter one countered by asking 'What do we look like?' Young Elsie began to work through her list. When she asked the type of their aircraft, the answer was 'a Halifax.' This was a strange answer, because the Americans had already been raiding in their own types of aircraft for months and some had been shot down. 'How many were in your aircrew?' 'Four.' The correct answer for a Halifax would have normally been seven, but the Luftwaffe had no four-engined heavy bombers and these men were making ill-briefed guesses. 'Why are you wearing khaki shirts? Are they your uniform?' 'Yes.' Of course, although evaders often acquired some very odd garments en route to them, both Elsies knew the R.A.F. uniform was blue, but Young Elsie had not so far been briefed on American airmen's uniform.

She quickly decided that she must consult Nemo before going farther down the question list in case this gave away too much. As usual, she asked the 'Americans' for the foreign money which airmen carried in their escape packs, explaining that they would be given money and the necessary papers for their journey, but they were very reluctant to hand it over. She also asked them to write down their names, ranks, numbers and aircrew functions and added their answers to her bag.

Robert went back for afternoon school. One man had asked to go to the 'cabinet' – an unusual word for the W.C., though 'Kabinett' in German can mean a closet – and then went out to look around the garden without asking permission. The Elsies both had worries about the 'Americans' which they quietly talked over as they washed up. Elsie thought Nemo should certainly be consulted but that they had nothing solid to go on. Always tolerant, she said that perhaps the men really felt ill and, as Americans, felt strange in an English home. She was not able to realise as fully as Young Elsie how unusual their answers had been because, even in the family, security was observed.

Then one of the men came to ask whether they could go for a walk for some fresh air. This was never allowed without escort as it was too risky, so Young Elsie suggested they should go into the garden; Elsie added that in the streets they might not be able to find their way back, to which the reply was 'Did you ever meet an American who couldn't find his way around?' The Elsies had no way of forcing them to stay in, so had to let them out and a few minutes later Young Elsie set off for the Canteen, carefully checking that she was not being followed by them or anyone else.

Looking back now, it is likely that the pair were as worried as the Elsies and needed to find a telephone to contact their superiors. They had come along the line successfully, trapping all the members they had so far met. Hangovers (from too much Dutch courage?) apart, they would already have been on edge when they arrived in Brussels, a nerve centre of the line. The unexpected encounter with two speakers of perfect English, one of them asking questions they must have realised they had probably not answered satisfactorily, had exposed weaknesses in their briefing, so they were now unlikely to move safely any further down the line as their orders would have required. Young Elsie was now off to report to her own leaders and might, for all they knew, return with armed Resistance men. They appear to have been told to play for time until reinforcements arrived and we have already seen Elsie's story of how they did this.

Young Elsie took the green envelope, note and the 'airmen's' written identity details straight to Greindl. He thought their writing might have signs of German script but could only suggest that the Maréchals should watch their guests closely and report any further doubts. Carrying his fine pigskin suitcase, lent so that she could take home food to help Elsie's unexpected catering problem, Young Elsie arrived home to be met by eight GFP men, including the 'airmen'. They said that something nasty had happened to her mother and now even more was going to happen to her. She was guilty of a grave crime and would be executed, but must talk and say plenty. One who was later to become the chief investigator of the entire family's case took her handbag, carefully examined each object in it including the certificate of work at the Swedish Canteen but put it and everything else back, returning it to her without apparently noticing anything which interested him.

Then interrogation started in earnest. Seizing the moment of greatest shock when she thought her mother was lying dead in the kitchen, they attacked with rapid, repeated questions, insults and menaces. Where had she been? Who had she been to see? Where was the money they had given her? (This seemed particularly important to them.) She stonewalled at first, to give herself a chance to work out her tactics. Then, as if giving way to their pressure, she said that she had been to do some black marketing. 'Where?' 'The Place de Brouckère' (a well-known Black Market centre). Then she conceded that she had spent all the money there. They took notes avidly but wanted at all costs to find out who was to give her the false papers she had promised to get. Now, to louder screaming and worse threats of other methods of making her speak, they added violent slaps on her face, alternating with offers of being well-treated if she did speak.

With all this going on, she fought to think how she might end it quickly in order to gain a breathing space when she could give more thought to some alternative to saying nothing. She and her mother were inescapably trapped; they could not deny the evidence. What mattered was not to compromise Nemo and the others in the line and to give them time to realise and react to what had happened. She managed to glance at her watch. It was half past four and a move occurred to her. She again acted as if she could hold out no longer and invented a story of a rendezvous with her chief at five o'clock at the main entrance of the Bois de la Cambre, a large park on the other side of the city. They took the bait.

After animated discussion, they acted quickly; one went to telephone and the two 'Americans' hustled her out of the house. 'Come, and if you try to run away, I'll stop you with this!' said one, showing her his pistol. He put it to her back, two others took her arms and they rushed through the nearby Parc Josaphat to a Tram 20 stop on the Boulevard Lambermont. The tram soon came; they ordered the passengers to the other end of the tram and at the St Michel roundabout (now the Place Montgomery) took her to a waiting black GFP car already occupied by four men. She was pushed inside to sit on the knees of one of them and the 'Americans' forced themselves in, too, making coarse jokes in bad French. Elsie, her head swimming, was more concerned with trying to gather her thoughts about what to do next.

The car stopped near the park entrance and she was told to stand at the supposed rendezvous where she would meet her chief, no doubt to receive her next orders and perhaps to collect false papers from him. They took up positions to watch, the two false Americans close behind her. Then, in the gloom of the drizzly November evening in the black-out, Elsie had to act her part. Once, she walked a few steps, ready to run off and disappear in the darkness, but was called back. An hour went by and an observant policeman came to ask what she was doing there. She told him to be careful as she was surrounded by the Gestapo and after glancing round, he took her point and walked on. After a second hour, the GFP realised that she had fooled them, threw her into a car calling her all the names they could think of and drove to the Gestapo office in the Rue Traversière.

There, her second interrogation, a long one, was carried out in the standard Gestapo method, by three men in turn, each with a distinct style. One, fat and breathless, shouted at her and predicted particularly unpleasant consequences unless she co-operated; the second was cold, polite and distant but more adroit and tried to catch her contradicting herself (but failed). The third, in another office, was simply brutal; when she stayed silent, he angrily shook her, hit her and twisted her arms behind her back. This went on until about ten o'clock when the questioning was stopped by a uniformed officer who came in pushing her father in front of him. She guessed from his pallor what had been his reception when he arrived home after his long day's work in Flanders. He knew nothing of the day's events, but as head of the family they were his responsibility and seeing him made Young Elsie realise even more the extent of the disaster.

They were both pushed into a car and taken to the St Gilles Prison. On the way, they managed to exchange a few words. 'Say nothing! *Tiens bon* [hold on]!' Georges whispered. She was never to forget the sounds of their first moments in prison. A warder, heavy boots echoing, led them down a long, badly lit corridor, noisily trailing a huge key along the grilles they passed, to the central point from which the different wings stretched and there he separated them. When she clung to her father, he laughed loudly but had the decency to turn away for a few moments before handing her over to another warder. She was thrust into an unlit cell and, feeling her way, tripped over a palliasse, on which she dropped, exhausted.

Alone at last, in spite of a blinding headache, she tried to calm down and collect her wits. She still had her handbag with some matches in it. She struck one and by its light found her work permit, tore it up and swallowed it so that the GFP would not now connect her with the Swedish Canteen. Her headache prevented her from having any sleep and, thinking all night long, she decided to keep to her first fiction.

Robert had endured his own evening's battle with the GFP. Two of them met him as he came home from school and took him to his bedroom, where he was allowed to sit on his bed as they interrogated him. He was very conscious that he looked young for his sixteen years and quickly decided to use his shocked state, exaggerate the stammer he had grown up with and play the frightened, naïve little boy who knew nothing. It worked, and after a time he was put in the back of a car, the escorts stupidly sitting in the front with the driver's window open. In fact he had been doing his own small job in the line that day. As sometimes happened, instead of using the Deceunynck corner shop route, his sister had given him a letter containing money, to take to school, to be passed to a fellow pupil, Martin, the son of Suzanne Wittek who, since her arrest, was still living with his grandmother and Aunt Ninie. Martin was absent that day, so the letter was still in Robert's pocket, but the GFP had not thought of searching a mere schoolboy. In the car, he stealthily worked his hand into his pocket, squeezed the compromising letter into the smallest possible ball and, after first thinking of pushing it behind the seat cushion, managed to throw it out through the open window just behind the head of the driver, who noticed nothing. Robert still reflects with amusement on the pleasant surprise that anyone curious enough to pick up and unravel that piece of litter may have had. Like the others, he was taken to prison and his own harsh interrogations were to follow.

Events at 162 Avenue Voltaire were not yet over. As time went on and Griendl heard nothing more from there, he and his colleagues at the canteen began to worry. Well after dark, probably in the early morning, one of his ablest guides on the French run, Victor Michiels, a 26-year-old lawyer, went to make a reconnaissance. He no doubt looked round with what care was possible, found all quiet and knocked on the door, to be challenged by the German watchers. Instead of raising his hands and talking his way out of it, he impulsively sprinted along the pavement towards the next street corner. The guards chased him, shooting, and he fell dead on the corner, where a graffiti-scarred plaque now marks the event.

The calamities stretched on. The following morning, as Michiels had not reported back to the Canteen, Peggy van Lier agreed with Greindl that as she and Michiels' sister were friends, she could safely pay a call on the Michiels and find the explanation. When she arrived, their house was also guarded by the GFP, who arrested her. They accepted her social call story, probably influenced by her striking good looks and her ability to talk with them in fluent German, despite her open horror when one of the security policemen apologised for having to break the news that they were at the Michiels' because they had been obliged to shoot her friend's brother. However, the young redhead's visit to a suspect household was not likely to be forgotten and Greindl decided to send her out to England, along with two more of his principal guides, Count Georges D'Oultremont and his cousin Edouard, before the GFP netted them. They obeyed unwillingly, but at least they could give I.S.9(d) a clear picture of recent developments.*

The next victim was Elvire Morelle, who arrived early by overnight train from France to visit Charles and stay as usual with the Maréchals. She was under no threat and had no more reason to visit the Canteen than Greindl had to know that she was coming, so she simply caught a tram and walked straight to the house to be added to the GFP's haul. After interrogation at the Rue Traversière, she was taken as a prisoner, not a visitor, to St Gilles.

The final event at 162 Avenue Voltaire was oddly trivial. The GFP were still there when M. Hunez had the misfortune to call, as he occasionally did if he had some spare bread ration stamps to give to Elsie. He was arrested and held in prison for several days before the Germans realised that he knew nothing to interest them.

---

* A year later, Peggy married Langley, Neave's senior officer in the section. Edouard joined the forces in Britain. Count Georges returned to survive eighteen adventurous months' service until liberation came.

INTERROGATION AND TRIAL

When her cell door opened after her sleepless night, Young Elsie was surprised and overjoyed to see her Mother coming out of a neighbouring cell alive and well. They were taken to the prison office for the formalities of criminal admission – identity details, fingerprints, profile full-face photographs and the hand-over of all their possessions, including jewellery, none of which they ever saw again. Elsie's account now becomes, by her standards, dramatically more outspoken.

Then followed a period of solitary confinement. We were placed in separate cells, 'au secret', that is to say, with no communication at all either with the outside world or with neighbours, no letters, or packets, or visits or privilege of any kind. The generality of the prisoners were lodged three in a cell, but those taken for working with the enemy were put 'au secret' until all the examinations were finished. Our daily walk was to turn round a long, triangular shaped yard, walled on two sides and barred on the other.

Our examinations were carried out by young, insolent non-commissioned officers. We were driven by car to the G.F.P. about 15 minutes from the prison and were left the whole day without food – while the examiners went home to dinner we were locked in the cellars. Every kind of treatment was tried to make us talk – promises alternated with threats. One moment they offered us white bread to eat, or the liberation of the other members of the family, and a little while after we were turned dizzy by blows or shaken like rats. E. endured sixteen examinations and was beaten on several occasions. A wireless was set going when there was a chance that the prisoner should cry or scream too loudly and the bathroom on the same floor was in frequent use to wash away the blood after the bad treatment. Many times have we seen women arrive in the cells after examination black and disfigured in the face with bloodshot eyes and unable to walk alone. They've told us how they'd been made to do gymnastics for hours until they dropped and then were kicked in the back or belly by the heavy army boots. One was stripped naked and her breasts burnt by lighted cigarette ends. Another was hung up by the wrists, another beaten with metal or rubber truncheons, and lifted from the ground by the hair and shaken until great tufts of hair were pulled out, another put into a bath with ammonia in the water and the head ducked under and so on – too numerous are the accounts to be told here. What the poor men suffered was much worse for they were generally sent to Breendonck, the camp of torture, to be made to speak. There were great dogs trained to attack the prisoners, starvation diets, dark, damp cells and the worst of cruel jailers to guard them. Luckily for us, B. was liberated after two months of detention.

By the time she wrote this, Elsie knew that her daughter had gone through experiences which could not be described to the girl's grandparents.

Young Elsie had soon realised that although they would both fight hard to say nothing, any stories she and her mother felt forced to tell during interrogation must match and she had already invented hers. The only time their paths were remotely likely to cross was during one of the short, daily, outdoor exercise periods described by her mother. On the guess that they might both use the same yard, she managed to write a short message on a sweetpaper she found in a pocket, hid it by the wall under a stone and with a hairpin she scratched on a brick above it 'Look here' (in English), with an arrow pointing down. Amazingly, Elsie noticed this, found the message and when she was next interrogated, confirmed her daughter's fiction. The result was a thorough search of both cells – fruitless as Elsie had, of course, disposed of the paper.

The third interrogation Young Elsie endured was brutal. The office windows were blacked out, the radio was put on at the maximum volume to hide her screams, a big lamp was set directly into her eyes, which she was ordered not to close, and she had to stand throughout. Having made sure that she was not wearing corsets, two interrogators stood behind her with batons and belts and she was told, 'The joke's over! You must tell the truth.' Seeing they were determined to be violent, she decided that this time she would empty her head and give only one reply, 'I've said everything.' The shouted questions went on and on. Each time she gave the same answer or shut her eyes, her back was beaten and the process was continued by relays of GFP for several hours until she fell to the floor. A pail of water and several kicks forced her to stand again and the process went on until evening, when she was taken back to St Gilles exhausted, unable to see clearly and hardly able to stand. In the cell, she could not eat, undress or sleep. The back of her dress was sticky with blood. That night, and for months afterwards, she could lie only on her side.

The next day, when she heard the number of her cell called, she knew that the nightmare was going to continue and in spite of herself, her teeth began to chatter, but on the way to the GFP office in the Rue Charles Degrelle she angrily fought to control herself, and succeeded. The interrogation began with a detailed statement in French, translated into German, that soon she and her parents would be guillotined, but if she gave them names and addresses, they would intercede in her favour at the trial. Then, the interrogator tried a new method. He stood face to face with her and stared into her eyes, trying to intimidate or perhaps to hypnotise her. She stared back with the same intensity without difficulty because the situation struck her as so absurd that, as it continued, her only problem was suppressing the growing urge to giggle. In the end, it won and she exploded, to be knocked down to the ground with a tirade of oaths.

Then, back to angry questions and more blows on her back until, exasperated, they took her to the bathroom where they sponged her face and tried to clean her up slightly as she was not capable of doing anything for herself. Finally, they took her back to the prison.

After several hours of peace in her cell, she realised that her nerves were being shattered and that before her imagination failed she should invent another plausible fiction. She finally decided that to gain some more time, she might use a conversation which she had overheard coming from the men's side, in which two prisoners were talking of naming a Resistance member 'Legrand'.* After another impossible night, she was again taken for interrogation and as the curtains were being drawn and the lamp fixed she said that she had a correction to make. She was allowed to sit down and ordered to say all she knew. 'I've lied. The chief's name is not what I first said, but another one.' As the typewriter rattled, she concocted a detailed description, with plenty of details about times, places and rendezvous and was spared more damage to her back, though the GFP still abused and spat on her. The interrogations continued;

---

* Henri Michelli (see p.40) invented a line leader called 'Albert Legrand' during his interrogation at this time, when he was in St. Gilles.

64

she was ill and weak but remained firmly determined to tell anything except the truth about the line and, especially, never to mention the Canteen. At one point, she was told that Victor Michiels had been shot when calling at the family house and was asked what she knew about him. At first, she denied knowing him but, after worrying in her cell, she again used her tactic of reluctantly yielding and in order to try to hide any possible trail leading to the Canteen claimed that he was her fiancé.

Meanwhile, the Germans were at work on her mother, who suffered her own nine interrogations and beatings. We have to deduce what we can about these from the deliberately generalised terms of Elsie's single paragraph, sparing her elderly parents' emotions. The chief investigator, Spiegelmayer, soon decided that repeated questioning and brutality would be wasted on Georges who obviously knew nothing of the false Americans and their reception, though he was still responsible for his household and would suffer the penalty due for whatever his wife and daughter had been doing. The Luftwaffe GFP were narrowly concerned with the airmen's escape line and never had the slightest suspicion of Georges' deep involvement in intelligence and secret army activities. He had, in fact, come home with a note of what he had observed in Flanders during the day but managed to put it into his mouth and eat it without being detected.

Robert was taken for many interrogations, beaten, kicked and knocked to the floor. Once, he was blindfolded, a revolver pushed between his shoulder blades and the interrogator howled at him, 'You have only three minutes to live! Speak! *Schnell! Schnell!*' One session began just as the prison evening meal was due, so that he was at a low point and it then lasted sixteen hours. He was in a large cell, usually with four men, in prison for a variety of reasons. One was a German Jew. The most annoying was a Black Marketeer who wept and bemoaned his likely fate all day long, but was freed after a fortnight. Another who was already in the cell when Robert arrived was very friendly and helpful, but was too inquisitive about what had brought Robert there to inspire trust. He was released and gave Robert his home address in Anderlecht. He left a scarf behind in the cell and after Robert was released, he went to the address to return the scarf, but found no one who knew the man; had he been a *mouton* – an informer planted by the GFP? The helpless, stammering child act proved convincing enough to persuade his captors that he was rather dim-witted and they would get nothing useful from him.

Towards the end of January 1943, Robert was ominously called out of his cell to take his belongings into the central hall of the prison and was astonished when a Feldwebel appeared and bawled. *'Mar'chal, frei lassen!'* He made his way across Brussels to his grandparents; his grandmother had pleaded for him to be allowed to live with her and his sick grandfather. His Uncle Marcel, who was not involved with any Resistance activities, had been bold enough to go to the Gestapo headquarters to argue for his release; he was not encouraged by the reaction: *'Ach! Mar'chal! Schwer! Schwer!'* [Very difficult!] Two years later, in the feverish atmosphere after Brussels was liberated, although by then he was in the army, some of Marcel's neighbours who knew he had visited the Gestapo denounced him as a collaborator and he had to clear himself before a military court.

Whilst the Maréchals were fighting their share of the battle on new and lonely sectors, Greindl was fighting his, to repair the damage done by the false Americans. He brought in new helpers but arrests continued and after a conference with Dédée early in January he spent very little time at the Canteen, hiring a flat for the document cache. Almost immediately, on 15th January, the line suffered its greatest blow: Dédée was captured, betrayed by an immigrant Spanish farm labourer when she was taking her seventeenth party of evaders into the Pyrenees. Greindl, refusing to leave behind his wife and children and pulling out to England, now went completely underground.

Not surprisingly she has not been able to date events precisely, but some weeks before this, there was a pause in Young Elsie's interrogations after her questioners had been more than usually boastful that they already knew all about her line. During this interval, although she was still *au grand secret* (in strict solitary confinement), another woman, a black market dealer, was put into her cell. Far from being a relief, she soon made herself intolerable by talking incessantly, and especially by being very curious about why Young Elsie was there. After a fortnight, she was taken away – leaving the suspicion that she was a Gestapo plant.

The respite from interrogation went on for several weeks and then one afternoon, to her surprise, Young Elsie was escorted out of her wing of the prison to a small parlour where she found, sitting at a table by the window, a priest whom she did not know. The door was locked and in a low voice, he said that he was supposed to hear her confession and give her the sacraments, but in fact was there to tell her that a large sum of money had been raised to obtain the release of the whole family He had already been to see Suzanne and Elvire and was going to see her parents. Out of his breviary, he produced a cigarette paper on which in Greindl's familiar writing was a message saying he had achieved the impossible. Before her arrest, she had overheard talk in the Canteen of a route for clandestine messages from St Gilles and of money to arrange releases, so she believed the news. Accepting a pencil and a clean cigarette paper, she quickly wrote a note beginning 'Dear Nemo,' assuring him that she had only told a pack of lies, interrogation had stopped and she was looking forward to starting their work again. She had just given her note to the priest when the door opened and the visit was over. She walked on air back to her cell.

Next morning, another surprise: she was indeed taken from St Gilles but it was to appear before Spiegelmayer yet again, to find him foaming with rage and hammering at her dossier with his fist, bellowing *'Alles ist Komödie!'* He gave an order in German transferring her parents to the dreaded camp of Breendonck (never in fact carried out) and gave her a pencil and cigarette paper shouting, *'Fous haller écrire à fotre cheff! Allez! écrifez!'* She sat, frozen. Then he shouted, *'Je fais vous dire ce que fous hallez écrire!'* and, holding her 'clandestine' message, read it out. The question came again and again, 'Who is Nemo?' Shaken, she made a big effort to stay calm, and did not answer. When the blows started again, pulling herself together, she said the last name she had given was false and went back to the first fictitious name she had given. A punch in the eye knocked her to the floor. She was kicked and pulled up by the hair, half-conscious Then, as the ritual was about to start again, boots were heard in the corridor, orders were shouted, doors slammed and Spiegelmayer was called out. After some time he came back and talked excitedly with the other interrogators, completely ignoring Elsie. Then to her relief, he ordered her back to prison.

Her morale shattered and in more pain than ever from more kicks and now a wounded eye, she was anxious to let Suzanne know of the leak in her message system. By now she had learned the old technique of talking with neighbouring prisoners by using a drinking vessel to speak into and listen to the heating system. By this route and the solidarity of the prisoners, she and Suzanne simultaneously arranged appointments at the prison dentist's. In the queue they exchanged a few words and written messages – Suzanne's three pages long. She already knew the message route had been detected and knew the name of the priest, Cracco. She was caught before she had destroyed Young Elsie's message, so they both had spells in unlit, unheated punishment cells, on bread and water.

Shortly after this, Young Elsie became very ill, with a high temperature and a badly infected eye after Spiegelmayer's punch. The German wardress took her to the prison doctor who surprised her by his civility, gave her drugs to treat the fever, looked after her eye, cleaned her open back wounds and then without being asked, made a report asking for the beatings to be stopped. To her relief, a period of respite from ill-treatment began, though she was now tortured by worry about her parents and Robert, of whom she could not get news, and by depression as she knew the Germans were closing in on the line and were no longer interested in her. She saw the prison filling up and slowly heard through the hot water pipes what was happening to members she knew. The list stays embedded in her mind. 'Jeanne Dupourque whose home was one of Dédée's first safe houses, then Dédée, Baron Greindl in February, Bidoul, Constance and Elizabeth Warnon; Yvette Guilmin who had taken over some of my work. Even Mme Greindl, the Baronne, was in a cell with her new-born baby. Then there was Mme Chaudoir and her servant Josephine; Mme Davreux of Namur and her two daughters Madeleine and Mercèdes and Mme Bachelave of that district.' To Young Elsie, pacing for hours in her cell, the line seemed destroyed.

There was an interlude when she was taken to a new investigator who claimed that on a particular date she had gone to Jeanne Dupourque's, to see Baron Donny. Donny (line name 'Père Noël' because he loved to visit evaders with presents) had joined in Frédéric De Jongh's time. Donny was brought in, having obviously been badly beaten and she was asked to identify him. Of course, she denied having ever seen him. This investigator did not persist and she returned without more ill-treatment to her cell.

At the beginning of April, she again heard her number being called. Her bruised back was still swollen, her eye was still not fully cured and on the way to the GFP, she once more struggled to stop trembling. She found the investigator with his feet on his desk from which he picked up an apple and threw it at her head. She ducked and he ordered her to fetch it. Her reaction was, in deliberate slow motion, to pick it up, sniff it as if were bad and roll it on to his desk. He bellowed like a defied schoolmaster, 'You dare to complain about bad treatment! We have special methods for bad girls like you, etc., etc.' and she prepared for the worst. However, this time the violence was only verbal. He showed her the typed statements in her dossier and said that if she wanted to be entitled to any clemency from the Tribunal, she would have to start again from A to Z and make it the truth this time. She refused and signed the file as it was.

'*Alles Lügen!* [All lies!]' he shouted. 'Now I'm the one going to tell you how it all works.' Then, in a childish revenge on this eighteen year old who had defied him, he boastfully set out in detail what the GFP had discovered about the line from Brussels, through Paris, St Jean de Luz, San Sebastian and Gibraltar to London, where he quoted names, addresses and telephone numbers of M.I. 9. He could not contain his delight in telling her of Dédée's arrest.

For the moment he had the mental effect he wanted, but Elsie was not going to show it on her face. The line's members only knew what they needed to know to do their job and although she knew more than most, much of this was quite new and she realised that they had been mere amateurs in the face of the Gestapo. If she had known at that minute that, in spite of everything, the line was going to be re-formed and continue sheltering and returning airmen to their squadrons, her morale would have been lifted, but she and her mother had to fight their private war for another two years before they could learn that.

The Trial
Elsie's dismissive account of the next event is perhaps all it deserved, even though the family's fate hung on it.

After four months of solitary confinement we were put three in a cell. Our examination was complete, and on April 15th 1943, G., E., our friend Nelly and myself were brought before the War Council of the Luftwaffe to be judged. It was quickly done. We were allowed only the official German lawyer to plead for us. He pleaded for G's acquittal by lack of proofs, but it was useless. All we could say was of no account, and we were all four condemned to death, with permission, however, to ask for grace. This we did and waited

69

in the prison of St Gilles always with the hope that this would be granted.

Young Elsie remembered every moment. A bus full of armed soldiers took the four to the military tribunal in a large old building on the Boulevard du Régent. A row of Luftwaffe officers in full uniform, sticks in their hands, assembled with heel-clicking and *'Heil Hitlers'* and then sat as black silhouettes in front of high windows through which bright sun shone on a perfect April day. After so long in prison, she preferred to look at the leaves just breaking on the trees outside. All the proceedings were in German which she only understood in a general sense, and opened with a lengthy demand that they, as very dangerous agents of a serious enemy of the Reich, must be punished without pity, in an exemplary manner with the maximum punishment. The defence lawyer was a Luftwaffe officer ('never saw or spoke to him before!') whose plea lasted only five minutes.

During the 'deliberation', the four were led out into a corridor and forbidden to speak. The Elsies enjoyed showing the scandalised guards their disrespect for the occasion by eating 'elevenses' – bread they had brought uneaten when they had been taken early from their cells. They had hardly time to finish before they were called back and after the same ceremonial as at the beginning, the officer acting as a judge ordered them to stand for the predictable verdict. The Tribunal found that none of them had any extenuating circumstances: her father was responsible for all that happened in his household; her mother was fully aware of having acted in support of the enemy; she, yet more, had the temerity to lie all through the interrogation. As for Nelly, she must have known what the correspondence she handled was about; finally, none had shown the least remorse, so the Tribunal had decided on the death penalty for each of them. There still remained the possibility of their pleading for grace, as no doubt they would do.

The whole trial had not lasted two hours and they were back in prison well before midday. It seemed incredible and ridiculous that they were by now condemned to death; even the prison guards were astonished and seemed to be looking at them differently – with pity and something like awe.

CONDEMNED TO DEATH

The prison regime at once completely changed. The next day, a German Jewess was brought to share Young Elsie's cell. She was the young widow of a non-commissioned officer of the Wehrmacht whom she adored and who had been executed for the racial crime of cohabitation with a Jew. After the Gestapo had arrested them by night, her husband was reduced to the ranks and shot at once. She was completely distraught and cried the whole time. Elsie tried to divert and encourage her, but nothing helped; she tried to kill herself twice. The first time, Elsie was able to stop her in time but the second time she managed to swallow a bottle of very strong cleaning fluid. Her stomach was washed out in time and she escaped immediate death but never returned to the cell and was sent to some unknown destination. Young Elsie was transferred to a cell for three prisoners where one of her cell companions was a trained soprano, who, from time to time, enchanted the others with an operatic aria. One evening, a German prison officer opened the door and asked her to sing Mimi's great aria; the whole wing was filled with her marvellous voice.

After a while, it occurred to Young Elsie to ask the warder if she could be put in the same cell as her mother as they were both condemned to death. He told her to make the request in writing to the Prison Commandant and to their delight and great surprise, it was granted.

Her mother describes the new routines.

We were then constantly moved about, never staying long with the same companions or in the same cell, for the Germans were afraid of us plotting an evasion. At 5 p.m. every day we were obliged to put our chairs together with our coats, dresses and shoes outside the cell to make sure we should not escape at night. All night long the light was left burning in the cells of the 'condemned to death' and the guardians did the round regularly to look thro' the spy-hole in the door. A little while after the judgement we were allowed to receive parcels of food and visits from our relatives. What a difference that made to our life in prison. News came in from outside that our demand for grace would surely be granted. Big influences – nobles, princesses and the Queen Mother herself – were working for us, so hope stayed high in our hearts, and all the insults, threats and punishments of the Germans could not lower the tone of our morale. Of course the brightest spots in our lives were the visits and the parcels. We, then, had means to pass little luxuries or necessities to less fortunate companions, and important messages passed in and out of prison under the noses of our keepers.

Robert was at last able to come to see the others and to collect their laundry. When he got home, it was his job to find the cigarette paper messages which they sewed into the hems of garments, before Esther or his grandmother washed them. Esther and the family put a lot of work and sacrifice into finding gifts for parcels and then had to queue outside the prison to have them searched. One of Esther's customers in the jewellery shop was Leichfeld, a prison officer who controlled visits and she somehow obtained a special visit in a small parlour instead of behind railings. There, in tight rolls which the Elsies had made, paper, colours, indian ink, brushes and pens discreetly changed hands, and were hung by a thread inside their skirts. Immediately after the privilege visit, they had to go to the large exercise yard which they now could use instead of the little triangles, walking one behind the other at arm's length in a large circle. All the group was ordered by a Wehrmacht officer called Zimmerman to stand in the circle round him for Swedish exercises. 'The funny part was that each time we did a knees bend, these rolls hung down between our legs and we couldn't stop laughing! We were lucky not to be caught.'

In the cells for month after month, with more and more line members condemned to death and joining them, they found relief – forbidden but all the more enjoyed – by embroidery and crochet, singing, playing cards – cut out of a cardboard box – and in Elsie's case by using the unaccustomed leisure to draw. Some of her small pictures of life in the cell were smuggled out and still exist, on show in the fortress at Huy.

On 7th September, to the great enthusiasm of most of the population, a big force of Allied bombers with fighter escort bombed targets in Brussels in daylight. Young Elsie was even more deeply affected than most of her fellow prisoners by hearing later that a single bomb on the barracks at Etterbeek had hit the block where Baron Greindl was imprisoned (in order to keep him away from

SOUVENIRS DE SAINT-GILLES

L'Hôtel
des
Patriotes

La Ratatouille

Bon Appétit !

the rest of the line captives) and killed him instantly.
Elsie tells what happened six weeks later.

The time, however, was getting very long. Every Friday a number of prisoners were called for deportation on the next day, and every week we wondered if it should not be our turn next.

Soon after, Berlin was submitted to a severe bombardment and Goering in anger refused the demands for grace that were awaiting his approval. We knew nothing of this, however, and the blow fell quite unexpectedly. One Tuesday morning we received our visit as usual. E. and G. and I saw the family and left each other in quite a happy and hopeful mood. The same evening G. was fetched out of his cell and passed the night, with other men of our case all condemned to death, in prayer and in writing his last letters to us. In the early morning of 20th October 1943 these eleven brave comrades were driven to the 'Tir National', singing patriotic songs, and in little groups of three or four they fell before the German bullets crying 'Long live Belgium! Long live England! Long live Liberty!'

The visit had been in the little parlour, where Young Elsie had previously met the priest Cracco. There she and her mother found not only Aunt Esther and her brother, Uncle Marcel but, as a complete surprise, her father whom they had not seen since the trial. During the conversation, he said in her ear, 'If you have the luck to get out one day, take good care of Mummy' and he told her not to forget that he had paid the fee for her studies at the Edith Cavell.

The Austrian chaplain of St Gilles, Mgr. Gramann, gave outstanding care to the group all night before their execution, including a celebration of Mass with one of them as server*. He saw that they were well fed early the following morning and accompanied them to the end. They all refused to be blindfolded as they faced the firing-squad.

During the previous evening, Georges wrote his will carefully, in pencil, on a simple sheet of paper which his children still have. Translated, the provisions of its seven short, numbered sections are:

---

* Mgr. Gramann is said to have ministered to more than 400 Belgians before their execution. After the war he asked whether he might be buried in the Tir National alongside many of those he had accompanied there.

1. He leaves his possesions to his children and their mother.

2. He appoints his brother Marcel as his executor and names two friends to assist him and present their accounts to him.

3. He writes, 'I desire England to adopt my wife and her children, if, without their being obliged to do so, it is their wish to give up their nationality.'

4. He asks for individual thanks to be sent by Marcel to those who have shown sympathy during the family's ordeal.

5. He asks for everything to be put in hand for his children to continue the studies they had already started or those they may wish to undertake.

6. He asks everyone concerned to accept his wish that life should continue normally without exaggerated regrets and that after the war nothing will be done specially for his body, which he wishes to be buried modestly.

7. He wishes that each year, annually, for ten years there should be a mass said for the repose of his soul on 21st June. [The anniversary of his marriage in England.]

He concludes, 'Written entirely with my hand at the prison of St. Gilles, 19th October 1943' and signs it as firmly as he writes it.

He also left a devotional booklet on the Stations of the Cross, given to him by Mgr. Gramann that night, on which he wrote '*A ma fille Elsie, en souvenir de son père qui l'adore.*' She still has it.

She remembers that a week later, three officers came into the cell she shared with her mother. They went to the back of the cell and stood to attention, this being the rule to avert escape attempts. The officer in the middle held and read out a document in German notifying Elsie of Georges' execution, which he then handed to her. 'I saw Mummy very straight, pale, with her lips trembling and I felt as if I had been knocked on the head. When the three men had shut the door, I took Mummy in my arms and she sobbed. There was nothing to do but cry together. Maybe our turn would come soon, but we were just indifferent.'

In November 1943 several of our line were called for deportation. Then we knew that our turn would come soon, but it did not make much impression now. What worse could happen to us now? Christmas 1943 came and found us still in St Gilles. Then on the eve of New Year's Day, our numbers were called.

At Christmas, Esther had moved heaven and earth to arrange with Leichfeld another unexpected visit in the parlour, the first since Georges' execution. Esther had just collected his belongings at the prison office and gave Elsie and Young Elsie their last letters from him. This set off Young Elsie into an outburst of uncontrollable revolt and she hurled herself at Leichfeld, who had arranged the visit and was standing in the parlour overseeing it, punching his chest and shouting 'Assassin!' He went pale and stepped back, but remained controlled and silent as the family brought her back to reason. She was very fortunate that he was such a decent man.

Elsie managed to pass out messages to the family before the transport left. Robert still has his, written in French on a cigarette paper in minute letters, using the smuggled Indian ink.

Mon très cher Bob,
Un tout petit mot pour te dire au revoir car je crois que nous allons bientôt partir. Je suis si triste Bob que Daddy est parti avant nous. J'aurai tant aimé rester ensemble jusqu'au bout. C'est possible que Elsie et moi partons samedi prochain mais naturellement on ne sais jamais d'avance. En tous cas je crois que nous serons vite de retour. Continue de bien étudier car c'est très important pour toi. Je suis si contente de voir que tu es devenu un homme - je pense tant à toi ... mon vieux, Bon courage et à bientôt Je t...
Elsie XXX   Mes meilleurs baisers   Mummie XXXXXXXX

Translated, it says:

> My very dear Bob,
>   A little word to say au revoir to you because I believe that we are going to leave soon. I am so sad, Bob, that Daddy has gone away before us. I would have so liked to stay together until the end. It is possible that Elsie and I leave next Saturday, but naturally one never knows in advance. In any case, I believe that we shall be back quickly. Continue to study hard for it is very important for you. I am so happy to see you have become a man. I think so much about you, old man. Good courage and see you soon. I [illegible]
> Elsie XXX   My best kisses   Mummie XXXXXXXXX

On New Year's Day, 1944, they left St. Gilles, wearing two sets of clothing and issued with a packet of food for the journey. The standard treatment, as always from now on whenever they were on transport, started as soon as they arrived at the station – armed soldiers; dogs barking; shouts of *'Los! Los! Schnell! Schnell!'*; forced to run to the train.

The ever-reliable Esther had somehow found out about their move and was there with Robert and his cousin Jean, waving 'Goodbye'. The train left immediately but they did not know that Robert had quickly boarded one of the normal passenger coaches to which their prison coach was attached. At Namur, he got out quickly to try to give them a parcel and they saw him running along the platform as fast as his legs could carry him, arm outstretched with his small parcel, as Young Elsie and he remember. 'You know, that was moving. I still see it, brother running with this parcel. He ran as hard as he could and the train was going and he couldn't see us, but we could see him. It was the last image we were to keep of Belgium.'

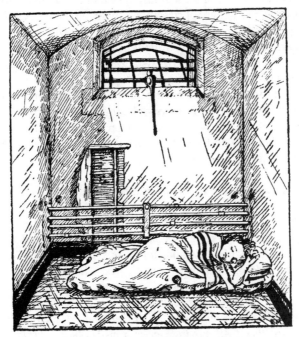

Elsie's sketch of Young Elsie smuggled out of St Gilles prison

NIGHT AND FOG

In 1915, the Germans had learned from the immense outcry folowing their execution of Edith Cavell that shooting a woman at the Tir National for helping escapers was a bad move. Georges Maréchal and his comrades had been shot for the same reason at the same place, but the SS had already perfected a more satisfyingly sadistic way of killing people they wanted to be rid of. This was to send them to labour camps, graded according to harshness, for slow death by under-nourishment, inadequate clothing, exposure to the weather, bizarre discipline, sleep deprivation and overwork. It had the added value of providing cheap labour for favoured industries or the SS business empire. As the finality of transport to most concentration camps dawned on the occupied countries, it became an even more horrifying prospect than the firing-squad or even the guillotine, which the Nazis had brought back.

It was the chosen fate for many resisters condemned to death, with the extra refinement of classifying them '*Nacht und Nebel*' (Night and Fog). This was an administrative category which meant final disappearance – death to the outside world, with no mail in or out, no parcels from family and friends and no answers to inquirers. In the case of women it had the advantage of avoiding any adverse publicity of the Cavell type. So the line members sentenced to death became 'NN' after they left Brussels and although they were for some time still under the German prison regime, the letters would appear on their cell doors as they started the tour of German prisons which Elsie begins to describe.

It was a small convoy of 'condemned to death', eleven women and eleven men. Our first halting place was Aix-la-Chapelle. What an impression of desolation and misery we received on entering Germany thro' streets of ruined houses to the old prison which had also been bombarded. Passing under the ruined walls, German prisoners made mute appeals to us for food – they knew that fresh arrivals from Belgium had Red Cross parcels in their possession. Once in the prison itself, we saw gaunt pale faces staring thro' wire gratings of cells lit by electricity all day long, for daylight never penetrated there. All our luggage was visited by the Head of the prison, a stout excitable person, who chose out of our belongings what she fancied for herself, so we were relieved of chocolate, cigarettes, soap, eau de Cologne etc. We were finally lodged seventeen in a cell, and in spite of the uncomfortable sleeping conditions and the awful food, the constant air alarms and the work of sewing buttons on cards, we managed to keep smiling and cheerful. After a week here, we were called for transport.

The discipline during the week at Aix-la-Chapelle was memorably relaxed. Cells were not locked and the freedom this gave to visit neighbours helped the line members to support one another's morale. Even a window without glass and a bomb-damaged section of open roof had the advantage of giving views of the sky and a ruined part of the town.

This word 'transport' brings up memories of being crammed into tiny cells of the police railway-wagons – seven being packed into a compartment for two – of perspiring, of being thirsty and tired and panting for air, of sleeping without covers on hard floors crowded together with prisoners of all conditions and nationalities, worried by bugs and lice in an awful stinking atmosphere. The sanitary conveniences consisted, usually, of bins or pails known as 'kubels' and which were continually in use night and day. From the stations to the prisons we were escorted by numbers of Gestapo armed with rifles and often accompanied by fierce dogs

So we passed from one prison to another, or to camp or cellars of the Gestapo. Each has left a special mark on the memory. Dusseldorf one of good food and of a few hours when we nearly forgot our misery in the contemplation of an enormous German co-prisoner of 120 kilos – she was there for selling butter on the black market. Shall we ever forget the sight of Frau Kromberg on the 'kubel'? She had such a tender heart, too; her face streamed with tears when she learned that we were all condemned to death. Cologne brings memories of night after night being called up to march out of the camp to an air-raid shelter and of the disinfection. Imagine about one hundred and sixty women stark naked in an enormous shower-bath hall, then passed into another large hall to dry (without towels) and to wait for an hour or so for the clothes to be disinfected with soldiers passing in and out from time to time. Franckfort, the sight of a man shut up in a bunker in the cellars, and bugs – especially *bugs. Nurenberg – lack of air – on entering our prison room we staggered backwards so thick and hot was the air. Here we met prisoners who had passed in Waldheim, which we had learnt to be our destination. To them Waldheim was 'prima!' so our spirits rose. Chemnitz and finally Waldheim an old established convict prison near Dresden*

This strange shunting of the party from one prison to another, often by very short distances, may have been to make sure that the line group was well and truly hidden in NN, but it seems more likely to have been a series of slots hastily found in an overcrowded system by the SS bureaucracy. It was made slower because the creaking railways, already heavily bombed, were trying to supply and move armies in Russia, the Balkans and Italy. Dédée De Jongh believed that being tried by a Luftwaffe court and classed N.N. with a number instead of a name hid her from the Gestapo and early death. Her Mauthausen record, unusually, has no entry in the space for her crime.

Journeys in Night and Fog

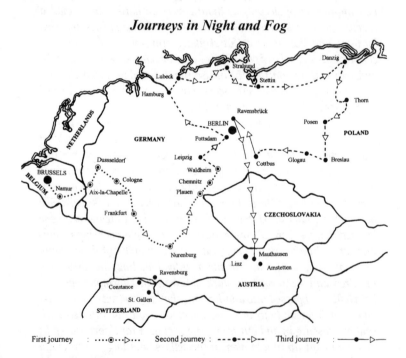

First journey : ····◉···▷····   Second journey : ---●---▷--   Third journey : ——●—▷—

80

Elsie omitted the worst details about Frankfurt. They arrived after dark and were led in dim light along a hall which was where they passed a small metal cupboard, or cage, which Elsie calls a bunker, perhaps thinking of a domestic coal bunker. The victim inside it was peering out, covered with blood and had no room to stand up or sit. As late arrivals, they and the rest of their party were simply pushed into a big room already full of prisoners in transport. The Elsies found a place to sleep on an old table, but the bugs made sleep impossible. 'Their stings were very painful – they were enormous ones, whoppers, and they were running all along the walls; you squashed them and they were full of blood.'

It is more surprising that Elsie does not mention a relatively comfortable stay in the prison at Plauen, between Nürnberg and Chemnitz, because there the party enjoyed the luxury of having a long shower bath and took advantage of the hot water to wash their hair and linen. They were given the not unpleasant work of wiring electric plugs and would gladly have stayed there. These last two stages were oddly short – only about 60 miles from Plauen to Chemnitz, for a single night's halt, when Waldheim was no more than about 25 miles farther on.

Entering Waldheim was like stepping into the middle ages. It was an old dilapidated building – cold, musty smelling – and the silence of the tomb everywhere. There was a moment of excitement. One of us had caught sight of one of our old companions of St Gilles, but this companion had had her hair shaved off! and had only dared to say in a hushed whisper, 'It's a hell!' It was not long before we were passed into the infirmary, where our hair also fell under the clippers – only two or three who had not long sentences escaped without having their heads reduced to the nakedness of a billiard ball. Then in the vestry we were undressed – all our clothes were packed away in naphthalene, and we reappeared in the convict costume – a cotton chemise and knickers (of what a cut!) – a short cotton jacket – grey stockings, wooden sandals and a triangular black head cloth. It was January and we missed our own warm clothes. I was now number 806 and the first fifteen days we spent in cells, stalking feathers. Then we were received one by one by the Directress who told us that as 'condemned to death' we were entirely cut off from the rest of the world and could not write or receive correspondence or parcels or visits. Then as fully-fledged convicts we were put into workrooms

81

– friends and relatives being carefully separated from each other. Some were put to work on munitions, others on electricity or in sewing or mending, making nets, cutting leather or sorting rags.

Young Elsie was, at this point, still able to feel outraged by the process of finally becoming a convict. 'We had to stand completely naked in front of the doctor and nurse and secretary and answer such questions as "Do you drink? Do you smoke? Have you been in prison or a lunatic asylum? Have you TB? Have you venereal disease? Any case of madness or murders in the family?"'

All the foreigners (about 300) slept in enormous attics under the roof in two-storied beds or straw sacks on the floor. There were many Czechs, some Yugoslavs and some French and Belgians. I and another were the only English-born prisoners there. Winter and Summer we rose at 5 a.m. We dressed, descended, stripped to the waist and washed in cold water very quickly. Then it was work – arbeit, arbeit – all day long during twelve hours with ten or twenty minutes interval for the scant meals, and a half hour for the daily walk, turning in a circle with carefully guarded distances in silence under the searching eye of the guardian.

These guardians were of two sorts – the professional, and those put there on war work. As a rule they were stupid, common women. The head of the institution, tall, badly dressed, with a deep, masculine voice, was however, an intelligent, capable woman and was ably seconded by the 'Walterin', a tall, red-headed but elegant and well-dressed woman, whose voice resounded in the prison from 5 a.m. till late at night. Under the direction of these two professionals the prison was ruled by an iron discipline. It was work and silence from morning to night. Only on Sundays were we allowed the relaxation of looking at a German book, and those with permission could write home. All we possessed, which generally reduced itself to comb, toothbrush, spoon, mug, towel, soap (if one may call it soap) and our daily bread ration, we carried constantly with us in a small linen bag. Woe betide the one who left this bag unguarded, for the bread vanished like magic. We were mixed with thieves, murderers, swindlers and criminals of all descriptions. One had killed her baby by putting it in the oven, another had put two children in a cupboard and set fire to it! Another, after killing her child had given it to the pigs to eat! Another had killed her fiancé by giving him a poisoned cake! Another had thrown a saucepan of boiling water over her mother-in-law! Another had beaten her twelve-year-old daughter because she refused to prostitute herself with an old man. Then there were many with three or four years of hard labour because they'd had a child (or perhaps only courted) with a Frenchman or a Pole, or because they'd shirked working in the munition factories. One had four year's hard labour and 7,000-marks fine for listening in to London.

At Waldheim, Elsie met 'the two Betties' for the first time. They had known only Young Elsie as the member of the line who brought airmen to their house. Elsie was introduced to Constance by Mme 'Nounou' Warnon who was in the same working party and from then onwards all three became firm friends. Constance still speaks of 'Polly' with affectionate admiration for her sense of humour in the worst imaginable circumstances.

During February and March we were never without snow. E was suffering from furuncles. I had diarrhoea and 'flu. Then E. caught scarlet fever and was very ill. She was looked after by the two criminals acting as nurses, roughly but cleanly and, nature helping, she recovered.

Elsie here once again hides the full horror. Young Elsie's 'furuncles' – the French word for boils which exists in English, though rarely used – were abscesses covering much of her back, left by her beatings. She was one of those sent to work in the Siemens factory where her task was to insert copper wire coils into metal cases. She had to clamp these shut by swinging a heavy lever with her right hand, and repeating this movement for long days agonisingly aggravated the abscesses under her shoulder. One day, she collapsed. Fortunately she was still in the prison system, so she was treated by the prison doctor.

At first, he thought her many skin eruptions might be caused by syphilis, so she was put in a room with two convicts who really had it. This rapidly improved her knowledge of life but not her health, and as the boils spread around her body the doctor changed his diagnosis. After treating them with ointment, he lanced the abscesses without an anaesthetic but with four prisoners holding her down and a pad in her mouth to bite. Although she screamed with pain, she remembers with a certain amusement that the doctor congratulated her for not weeping. The discharge from her open wounds soaked through the palliasse to the floor, enraging the prisoner 'nurses', who beat her afresh. The doctor then found that she had scarlet fever, so fortunately he put her into isolation and treated her septic condition with sulphonamides. Her skin peeled, she lost her hair and became very thin, but after three-months' illness she rejoined her mother.

It was in the Spring of '44, and a great nervousness and expectancy of invasion was felt by prisoners and guardians alike, but the days and weeks passed with only news of tremendous air-raids to break the monotony. One morning, the news flashed thro' the prison (let out by the guardian) that the Allied forces had landed in France. That evening it required all the resources of the managing directress to calm us, and from that moment snatches of songs were heard in an undertone and little groups gathered in the lavatories to discuss the latest news.

One morning towards the end of June, Elsie and I and our friend Nelly were called in the midst of our work for transport. We were searched and dressed in our civilian clothes and for three days were kept in great secret in a cell apart. From time to time, prisoners were called for transport and for those condemned to death it generally meant Dresden and decapitation. Many were the conjectures that we made, and constantly the idea of decapitation recurred in our minds. To be shot seemed to be almost agreeable at the side of that. However, we were relieved to find that our train, when at last we started, left in the direction of Leipzig. At Leipzig we passed again thro' the disinfection. We were now used to being naked on all possible occasions, so we derived no special thrill this time. After being well washed and disinfected we were put into crowded cells swarming with bugs!

Elsie totally omits the worst part of the stop in Leipzig. The 'cell' was a wooden barrack and the prisoners were driven into it, packed so tightly that they only had room to stand. It was a hot summer night and there was no ventilation whatever. The Elsies, as ever, kept together with Nelly. As the place became more and more stifling, a very big Russian woman had some sort of fit or siezure, and collapsed on top of Elsie. Young Elsie frantically summoned up all her strength, pulled her mother up and with Nelly fought through the crowd towards the door, which she hammered, calling for help. None came. When guards finally opened the door in the morning it was for the usual '*Schnell! Schnell!*' forced run to transport and Young Elsie and Nelly had to half carry Elsie, who could barely stand, for the long journey to Pottsdam during which she slowly recovered.

Then we were sent to Pottsdam. The prison was a horror. Nelly slept on a small table and E. and I on the cement floor under the table and in the morning we were sent on our way to Hamburg with no food to eat for all day. But in our great misfortune we often had little strokes of luck. Passing thro' the province of Mecklenberg a woman just arrested was put in with us. She heard us speak of being hungry and immediately brought out of her bag a packet of sandwiches of good bread and butter and sausage and even a small box of strawberries freshly gathered from her garden. She spoke both English and French and turned out to be the Countess of M. Half her family was fighting for the Germans and the other half for the English and she was arrested for having been to pray on the tomb of a Canadian pilot.

They never again saw the Countess of Mecklenberg. They found entire districts of Hamburg ruined by air raids and half the prison had also been destroyed.

After a week in Hamburg we were sent to Lübeck which should have been our destination , but counter-orders had been given and no foreigners were to be kept in Lübeck. It was the convict prison of Lübeck and very different from Waldheim. There were large corridors, polished and shining floors, two-windowed cells with four beds, very clean, running water and a real bathroom – alone for a quarter of an hour – what a luxury for us who were always herded together like beasts. It was a model institution of its kind and we might have been comparatively happy there if it had not been for hunger. A small block of bread (for all day) and a little coffee in the morning and a bowl of watery soup at mid-day, and a little coffee in the evening was the daily transport ration. We were given trousers of dead German soldiers to take to pieces. They were often bloodstained and dirty but this work procured us a ration of syrup and liver sausage.

This transfer from the south-east corner of Germany to the north-west corner must have been deliberate at a time when the rail system was overburdened and under day and night air attack. The reasons for it and for the rapid counter-order can only be guessed. What followed was an even stranger series of inhuman improvisations than those of the journey from Brussels to Waldheim. Elsie studiously avoids giving details of her own sufferings, but leaves no doubt that this second odyssey inflicted far worse suffering on the already weakened victims.

Once more we were sent on our travels. Our destination was Cottbus, south-east of Berlin, but owing to the bombarded railway centres we were directed along the Baltic coast of Germany and down thro' Poland. We stopped a night at Stralsund in awful cellars of the Gestapo; then arrived in Stettin. The SS chief here was the best example of the perfect brute both in appearance and in manners that we'd met in Germany, and we've met some! Every day he marched the women four abreast around a small yard, commanding them to sing songs of the 'Hitler Jugend'; those who did not obey implicitly were sent direct to the cellars. We heard stories here of Polish prisoners being given the choice either to hang their companions, or else to be hung themselves.

The 'awful cellar' at Stralsund had only bare, wet earth floors and a large plank on which a dozen prisoners had to rest as best they could They were sent on to Stettin having been given nothing to eat or drink. The sadistic SS officer at Stettin was assisted by like-minded wardresses, one of whom so disliked the foreigners that she earned them three days' deprivation of food by moving their straw palliasses out of line before the inspection. In fact, they only suffered by being sent on transport once again the next day without food.

After Stettin we travelled to Danzig. Passing through the port of Gotenshaven we had a tiny glimpse of the masts of ships and imagined we smelt the sea air. The little we saw of Danzig gave us the impression of a fine city, but the filthy barracks we slept in made us happy to be sent on to Thorn in Poland. We arrived after that in Posen, memorable for the bug-hunts. In the morning they ran in great quantities up the freshly whitened walls, and guardians joined us in the hunt.

At least they were given small portions of bread for the journey from Danzig and as it was in normal passenger carriages they were able to enjoy looking at the landscape, with ripening cornfields and forests and the occasional peasant woman at work. This was only an inadequate distraction from their hunger, which meant that the only memory either of the Elsies retained of the night at Thorn (now Torun) was that there were peas in their 'meal' of soup.

Then came Breslau. We were packed in an ancient 'Home for young Jewish girls.' The formerly rich home was filthy and deteriorated, infested with vermin, and the female guardians, painted and powdered, smoked cigarettes all day. There we had to unravel old socks. There was a Yugoslav woman with a 15 days old baby. She had worked digging trenches until a fortnight before the birth of the child and had, when it was born, had to wrap it in paper. Thanks to a guardian and fellow-prisoners, the child was soon clothed, but neither child or mother received the slightest drip of milk. We found the mother trying to give the child jam and coffee with a spoon and all the linen had to be washed in our sink with cold water and no soap. Again, in transport, we spent a horrible night at Glogau on the Oder, and then arrived in the convict prison of Cottbus.

For the 'horrible night in Glogau', the party was again packed into a cell far too small for them, without ventilation, without food, and left to sit exhausted on the floor in water leaking from an old, broken WC, to which prisoners clambered over one another all night. For the first time, Young Elsie saw a tear running down her mother's cheek. She felt her physical resistance diminishing, she had a persistent cough and she was anxious about what might be happening to Robert. Victory might be coming but would it be too late for her and her daughter? Secretly, Young Elsie was not sure either, but she tried to encourage her mother to hold on, minute by minute, hour by hour, day by day and not at any price to let the Germans win. At Cottbus, their party was able to regain the support of the rest of the line.

Passing the entrance gate and crossing the courtyard, we heard our names called and looking up, we discovered the faces of some of our companions of Waldheim peering thro' the window bars. As we found out afterwards, all those condemned to death had been transferred from Waldheim to Cottbus in one day, while we had taken nearly six weeks to come. Here we were again stripped of all our belongings, dressed in uniform and became numbers once more.

The next day at the daily walk, how happy we were to see all our friends again – not only those from Waldheim, but also others who had been in other parts of Germany – quite a huge assembly of 'condemneds to death'. Many of them had been kept four months continually in handcuffs. The work here was chiefly making plaits (for sandals, bags etc.) out of maize leaves. We were each supposed to do fifty metres a day, but produced generally five to ten metres a day! The Directress, a small insignificant person with short cut hair, was nearly always in trousers. The discipline was poor, and as in all prisons the hours were long and the food short. We had soups of dried swede, turnips and of cucumber. Our hunger was never satisfied; some picked up acorns to eat or cabbage stalks from the rubbish heap and the mealtimes became all-important. It was summer and we suffered from heat and vermin, especially those who were lodged seven or eight in a cell. We were neglected rather than badly treated – for instance, left four months without a change of linen. There was talk that we were to be moved, and there was news brought in by fresh prisoners that the Allies were advancing. We became more and more difficult to manage and the guardians preferred to cut out our daily walk altogether rather than have the bother of keeping us in order. Cutting down the food was the only effective punishment; that only was serious for us for we were becoming weaker and more and more like skeletons every day.

The Elsies shared yet another airless and overcrowded cell with Nelly and Hettje, a Dutch companion who had become their friend since they met at Lübeck, and four others. The 'huge assembly' of NN women, condemned to death, included resistance and political prisoners from many occupied countries, which was why they felt themselves exerting a corporate strength against the prison officers and were so difficult to control.

Those who had been on the nightmare tour of Germany were in a far worse state than those who went straight from Waldheim to Cottbus. The principal subject of conversation became the *nachkost*, the small left-over after the evening soup had been measured out, which went to the cell beyond the last to be served its ration. One day on the daily exercise walk a ration of bread fell to Young Elsie's feet from an upstairs window. It was from Elvire Morelle, who was herself suffering from hunger oedema of the legs. Young Elsie, no longer young, still calls it the best present she has been given in her entire life.

After being soaked in water, the pile of maize leaves for the plaiting the prisoners were supposed to do was thrown into the cell, where there already was no room. They entertained themselves by making dolls and slippers with them. Constance remembers that Elsie's expertise in producing particularly amusing dolls did a great deal to keep up spirits. At the end of one week, when all the work was taken out of the cell, a defiant old French lady showed her ten centimetres and shouted *'Deutschland kaput!'* She was put immediately into the punishment cell, singing at the top of her voice, 'La petit diligence, sur le chemin de France, s'en allait gaiement, gaiement!' To occupy herself, she was chasing the bugs with an old sandal and knocked down a shelf full of crockery. For that, she was punished by deprivation of food for eight days and died exhausted a little later.

In late Summer, 1944, when the scarcely credible victory news came through from the west and the rumour spread that Brussels and Paris were liberated, the cell groups cheered and sang and did an Apache dance, earning three days without soup or exercise.

As the SS faced defeat, they avenged it on those of the Allied victors still within their power. The worst of the prison system having failed to break them, they would use their final weapon, the extermination camp for women.

Rumours of leaving Cottbus became more insistent – even of being sent to a camp under the direction of the Red Cross (no more under the SS) and even of being liberated. One day in November* they started sending us away in groups of forty or fifty at a time. We again received our own clothes and were again on transport. Where to? The house-mother assured us we should have a few surprises. She was right. Our destination turned out to be the concentration camp of Ravensbrück in the marshland district between Berlin and the Baltic.

---

* Plisnier-Ladame, from Ravensbrück records, gives the dates of these transports' arrival there as 15th, 21st, 22nd and 23rd November and quotes 'Constance' as giving her arrival as 23rd.

The Elsies' transport party was forced to wait for a long time on the station platform at Cottbus. On the platform opposite was another transport party of men, including a young blond Norwegian who was still fit enough to see Young Elsie's attractiveness and struck up a conversation with her in rough English. He asked her to write to him after the war and told her his name and home address in Trondheim. Later experiences meant that she forgot them – and she still wonders whether this was a pity. Their brief encounter was ended by the arrival of the SS with their dogs, their superiority, their hatred and their shouting, lining up the prisoners as usual in columns of five and whipping them along with no concessions to the lame or sick. *'Schnell! Schweinhünden! Links, rechts, links, rechts!'* Discipline was being restored.

CONCENTRATION CAMPS

Ravensbrück

At the entrance to the huge Ravensbrück camp, there was a long wait, during which the newcomers began to shiver from cold rather than fear, facing the double entry barrier, with its sign *'Arbeit macht frei'*. On either side stretched a double fence of barbed wire in front of a high wall. From the top of towers, sentries kept a strict watch, ready to shoot.

A drizzling rain added to the gloomy aspect of our arrival in the camp and a shudder went through us as the barrier shut behind us.

Once inside, Young Elsie was first struck by the shining blackness of the wet ground covered by coal dust, but then alongside one of the dark green painted barrack blocks she saw an open cart pulled by women. 'I couldn't believe what I saw. Piled in anyhow were bodies, naked, thin – just bones – with the limbs dangling everywhere, with mouths and eyes wide open, abandoned in a miserable death. That's what we saw when we arrived.

Afterwards, we were to learn that this was the cart that would pick up the bodies of those who died at night and were deposited at the entrance of each *blok* each morning, to be taken to the crematorium. But it wasn't the moment to go into meditation because the reception committee leapt on us. Barking, screaming, insulting us, warders called *offizieren* [SS of all ranks] took us running towards an enormous tent – it looked like a circus tent – there to leave us until the evening.'

We were directed to a huge tent erected in the centre of the camp. As a rule all new arrivals passed the first night or so in this tent, but many spent weeks there, too. There were about 1,600 Hungarian Jewesses in the tent – lying or sitting in filth on the ground. They had been taken by the Germans before the advancing Russians near Budapest, to dig defence trenches, and finally arrived here by forced marches with little or nothing to eat; those who could not follow were simply shot down. One or two mugs of soup improved our morale a little for we were starving.

The soup arrived after night had fallen. Constance urged her companions to drink it as quickly as they could so that they could get second helpings. It was so hot that it burned Young Elsie's throat but none the less she was glad to gulp down more.

The awful spectacle of this tent is engraved on our minds for ever. Some were ill or dying, others sleeping on blankets in pools of wa-ter, others talking, eating or groaning. A row of utensils of various shapes, pails, jugs, cans etc. at the back of the tent took the place of lavatories. Imagine the state of these towards the morning, over-flowing and the smell thereof. We spent the best part of the night walking up and down trying to keep warm, but in the end were forced to lie on the damp ground and sleep an hour or so.

The next afternoon we were lined up outside the 'baths'. There were hundreds of Jews to pass before us. As they entered they were obliged to leave all their baggage in a tremendous heap outside the building. It was raining and bags, sacks of clothing and food were thrown pell-mell in the mud. We waited in the beating rain and it was midnight before our turn came. We were stripped of every-thing except corsets and shoes; our bags were thrown open and all our things chucked out and trampled on. We were just allowed to keep spectacles, combs and toothbrushes. After the bath we were given a thin chemise, knickers, dress and coat – old clothes of those who had passed before us. The result was often ludicrous and when one of our companions (a countess) donned the gypsy's outfit allot-ted to her, we were forced to laughter. E. and I found ourselves the possessors of short Russian jackets, rather cold for the legs, but being padded protected the chest rather well.

Through all the searches and confiscations so far, Elsie and her daughter had each kept her own last letter from Georges, but these, their greatest treasures, now disappeared for ever. Young Elsie was even more angered by the pitiful sight of 'women of all ages, espe-cially the eldest ones, with their poor fleshless bodies with empty skins, trembling with cold and fear, brutalised, being forced to run like young ones up to the showers! The old ladies of our group, dignified and of good education, had no right to respect. Just the contrary, they were regarded as useless. Poor Mme Davreux, so thin, Mme Chaudoir, Mme Van Kampenhout, these were really old peo-ple – Mme Davreux was eighty. "*Schnell! Schnell!*" We went through the collective showers without soap, without towels, pushed into an antechamber – a sort of drying room – where we were shivering and then into a big passage where tables were lined with clothes in piles taken from other disappeared prisoners.'

The clothes had been disinfected, but not laundered. On the back of each jacket was painted a white cross as an aiming mark in case the prisoner ran away. Each prisoner had to sew a triangular patch on the top of the right sleeve, of a colour showing her category: red for 'politicals' included resistance members; black for antisocials; green for ordinary lawbreakers such as thieves; and yellow for Jews – the lowest ranked. The number, the only official identity of each, was on a tape to be sewn on the jacket front – 84887 for Elsie and 84888 for Young Elsie.

The extraordinary thing of the camps was the comparatively few Germans used to run them. The police was almost entirely done by Poles and I must say they did it very effectively. They had suffered themselves and seemed to wreak their vengeance on us. What shouts and threats would not do, the schlag would do. How many times have we not seen their victims fall on the ground under their blows?

We were sent to our 'block'. There were 32 blocks in the camp and the chiefs of the blocks were often Poles. The dormitories were filled with wooden constructions of three-storied beds separated only by very narrow gangways, and we were put two or three in a bed. The refectory was originally used for meals, but with the over-population there were beds there too. The soup was served there, but only a minority could be seated at the tables, so it was the general rule to eat in our beds.

Young Elsie described their introduction to their *blok*. 'There was an amazing, overcrowded confusion. Shoved about in all directions, sworn at in different languages, you had to make your way across the entrance and *waschraum* before arriving at the dormitory, where you had at all costs to find a place in a three-storey bed, furnished with a dirty palliasse. You had to push when you arrived there and argue and shout like all the others to make your way. Finally, we had a bed for three on the second level over one of the bunks. No question of leaving whatever you had there – its theft was certain. The bunks were ranged in groups of three or four and you had to climb down and pass on all fours on other beds to get to your place and that caused a lot of shouts. You could only get through alley-ways one at a time and this was another source of shouting.

The soup cans arrived at the refectory, where you had to queue to get some very off-colour liquid in which sometimes a swede floated. We had a bowl for the soup, hanging from our waist; we always had to hang it so that it was not stolen, or lost. There too, you had to fight; nobody wanted the top of the can because it was too liquid. There was never any meat or potatoes and yet good smells came from the kitchen, proving that some were privileged, but not our *blok*. We had to queue to receive our ration of black bread (containing sawdust) and it was a sixteenth part of a loaf – that's one slice. In the refectory at Christmas, 1944, a very tall Canadian woman, with legs swollen with hunger oedema, started singing carols in a very sweet voice. Two days later, she died. Eating in the *blok*, we were everywhere, in corners, alongside the walls and cupboards, on and under the tables. At least there was a fire – one for the whole *blok* that gave a little heat at the ends of the dormitories, which were icy cold with broken windows. We were supposed to be 250 in each dormitory; in reality we were 500 on each side. We slept fully clothed with some goods under our heads, to prevent them from being stolen.

Each *blok* had a head called *blokova* and each sleeping room – one at each end – had a *stubova*. Our first *blokova* was a cultivated person, a Polish princess, too civilised for the function. Her discipline left something to be desired, so she was replaced by a Russian woman soldier, Ivanova, of glacial style. She was built like a Frigidaire! Ordinary, hard and brutal, with a terrible voice. In the morning, when we were sound asleep, the siren howled lugubriously and we only had a few minutes to jump out of bed, re-button ourselves and run in a terrible mess, to queue up in front of a row of lavatories without doors, in the filth and smell to make you want to throw up of all those who had uncontrolled diarrhoea; many had typhus. The *blokova* pushed us with a truncheon, screaming *"Los! Los! Schnell! Appel! Weitergehen!"* She was very brutal. In the refectory, if you were quick enough, sometimes you could manage to have just a little coffee in the mug we had also at our waist, but everywhere it was an enormous pushing to get out.'

At 5 a.m. we were up and turned out of the blocks for the 'appel' or roll-call. We had to arrange ourselves in the appointed places in

*rows of ten and wait for the 'Offizieren' to pass and control the
numbers. If there was one too many or too few in the total of over
50,000 women the whole camp had to stand waiting until the error
was discovered. Every day, in rain, snow or wind we stood under
the stars and under the glare of electric lamps until the dawn broke.*

The details of the crazy rituals of *Appel* were frozen into Young
Elsie's memory, 'Drawn up in a precise place of the Lagerstrasse,
we each had a determined place, ten by ten, the groups at arm's
length apart in front and on the side. The order had to be perfect;
nothing had to come out of line and during the long inspection,
however many times repeated by the women *offizieren*, the feet had
to be in line, arms along the body and looking straight in front, or
the *schlag* went down fiercely with oaths, "*Scheissdreck! Schweinhund!
Dumkopf!*" As soon as they went, we started beating our feet and
arms so as not to get frozen in the night, because it was cruelly cold
and we had not enough clothing. The frost pinched our fingers and
toes, and we were blue with cold. I hated clear skies, full of stars,
because then the cold was more intense still.

Sometimes, one of our companions fell over and we had to pull
the body on one side and re-form the ranks immediately. During
that time, in the barracks, those that had died at night were pulled
into the *waschraum* and from there to the outside of the *blok* to be
counted. We often waited a very long time – from three to four hours.
We had often to get up at four o'clock. When the shape of the black
pines showed against the light of the coming day, finally, we were
told of the arrival of the SS. With an enormous *"Achtung!"* we had
to stiffen up in a perfect attention position. They arrived, arrogant,
superior, boots stamping, making their coats fly about them. They
counted us – *siebzig, achtzig, neunzig*, ten by ten. They counted us
and they counted us and recounted us several times. If the count
was not right, we had to wait without moving for hours at a time. It
lasted like that every day in spite of freezing fog, beating rain, cold
wind, freezing cold snow, storm, every day whatever the weather.
We wondered if it was possible to be colder, more hungry. Of course
it was possible because human resistance is unbelievable.'

*After the 'Appel' there was the work or 'Arbeits Appel'. We had to
arrange ourselves on the 'Lagerstrasse' and then there was the march
past. All those who had no fixed work, the 'Verfügbar', were liable*

to be pounced upon and sent to work on various duties such as digging trenches, pushing carts of goods, or refuse, or corpses, carrying heavy loads of coal, chopping wood, loading and unloading railway trucks. Just outside the camp trucks arrived bringing goods of all descriptions – furniture, clothes, porcelain, silver, mattresses, linen, utensils of all sorts – all goods plundered from Poland, etc. We were obliged to unload these, sort them out and pack them in large halls. There were here good opportunities to take possession of woollen garments, knives, spoons and other little luxuries, but of course it required a little ingenuity in passing them for we were searched and sometimes stripped naked for the search.* What astonished us was the awful waste, for fine linen and articles of value were left rotting together with rags in huge piles in the open air; when we moved them under the snow they were hot and steaming with fermentation.

Those who had any qualification as doctor or nurse were employed in the infirmary. A great number were employed by Siemens in munition factories attached to the camp and received better treatment.

The privileged columns also included those working inside a cement factory, and in the camp offices. Then there were those working in the kitchens and personal service to the SS who might manage to filch extra food and were at least in rather warmer places than the lower orders, who were put into columns that were *verfügbar*. These were the French speakers and politicals – the NN – who ranked just above the Jews. At the very bottom were the Gypsies.

After the 'Appel' it was a great rush of all those not taken for work to enter the block and creep into bed to try and get warm. The bread ration for the day was generally distributed about 11 a.m. Then at midday came the soup – nearly always of swede turnip, sometimes cabbage. Our first gesture on receiving the soup was to turn it to see if there were no pieces of meat, but these were very rare for the soup had passed thro' other hands before reaching us. There was a

---

* Mme Jeanne Dupourque managed to exchange her thin coat for a Harris tweed overcoat and switch her triangle and number tape. She did the same for Elvire Morelle.

tremendous leakage with the food; whole kettles of soup were stolen from one block by another.

If one prisoner disobeyed the rules, the whole block was punished by a pose of four or five hours or more out in the cold. Our greatest sufferings were from hunger and cold and still those who had been there a long time told us that conditions were greatly improved – that formerly dogs were trained to jump at those wearing the convict uniform, that there were three appels a day and that punishments were much more terrible. Now there were not enough striped convict dresses to go round, so other coats and dresses had to be marked with a big white cross on the back.

The most redoubted illness was dysentery. It was a general rule that new arrivals caught this almost immediately and one saw them change in a few days. Medicine was very scarce and it required 40 degrees Centigrade of fever to be admitted to the infirmary. The bodies of those who died in the night were stripped and put on the floor of the washroom until the next day when they were collected by the cart to be taken to the crematorium. No film nor book nor description can give the real atmosphere of Ravensbrück; the awful smells of dysentery and of the crematorium are missing. The acute sensations of cold and hunger and the glimpses of suffering and dying faces; the handling of naked dead bodies like refuse; the commerce for bread and clothes; all this cannot be pictured. It must be lived to be realised.

Young Elsie records the story of one casualty. 'One day when we had to rush out for *appel* in the morning, somebody in a lower bed pulled my skirt and held it. I bent over and saw a very old lady with completely white hair, with terrible fever – in fact, she was dying. She wanted to say something and so I put my ear to her mouth and could understand her. She asked me to tell her son that *Maman* was dying bravely for France, that I was to tell him that she loved him above everything and that he must keep on trying to be a good boy. I tried to hear her name but I couldn't hear anything more that she said. Then I got a knock with the truncheon from the *blokova* because I had to be out and I was standing there, so I had to go out. When I came back hours later, I found her bed empty, so her body had been taken away. I never knew who she was, so I could never pass on her message.'

At the beginning of February the old, the thin and the ill were sorted out. We passed in a long queue, stark naked before the doctor, who put the medical cards on one side of all those picked out as unfit. All these were sent to a camp, a 'Jugend Lager' as they called it, a few miles from Ravensbrück, to be specially looked after. This special treatment turned out to be starvation, no blankets and long poses in the cold. Several died and all those who remained were sent on transport – the black transport. None of those in that transport have been heard of since. Everything leads us to believe that they were exterminated in the gas chambers. I had been chosen to go to this 'Jugend Lager', but thanks to a doctoress whom I'd known in the prison of S. Gilles who changed my medical card I was able to escape it and remain with E.

The 'doctoress' was Mme Goldschmidt, a Jewess who had beeen in the next cell to Elsie in St Gilles. They had talked and got on well there. Now she was standing next to the German doctor who was doing the selection and recognised Elsie. The Elsies never saw her again but about twenty years later, Elsie met someone in the south of France who said that she knew Dr Goldschmidt, and that she was alive and still practising. The elderly Mme Chaudoir of the line was sent to the Jugend Lager and never came back. Mme Davreux died in Ravensbrück and one of her daughters, Madeleine, came to ask Young Elsie to carry her to be put on the pile of corpses. 'She was this lady, eighty years old. They had shaven all her hair – she was a very dignified lady with long hair down to her waist. I took her by the feet and she took her by the shoulders and I said to myself, "That's your mother, your dear mother, and there's not a tear, not a sign of sadness in your face, nothing. That's what we've become – without emotion for anything any more. Is that what we've become?" And we got her down there and that was that. She lost her mother and I still had mine.'

The Russian advance to the Oder brought about rumours that Ravensbrück was to be evacuated. A bombardment of the electrical installations put the camp several days without light, and there were often no more roll-calls in the morning – a thing never heard of before. Those working in the forest outside the camp heard the cannon booming in the distance.
There was a certain number of Polish women in our block known

to us as the 'lapins' [rabbits]. These had served as experiments to the German doctors. Some had had bones removed, others operations on certain nerves or muscles. There were many women and even Jewish children who had been sterilised. E. had Polish friends and one day she was upset, for one of her friends had been condemned to death and executed by being hung by the feet in the chimney of the crematorium.

This is Young Elsie's account of two brief friendships with Poles. 'In the *waschraum*, there was a tap in the middle and others round the side. Everyone was trying to get water and we had to walk over corpses put there in the night. I noticed one woman that had one leg dangling behind her, completely paralysed, and said "Can I help you? What was it?" She said, "Oh! I was one of the rabbits." They did experiments on the nerve fibres and had taken out the whole sciatic nerve. Others were inseminated because they did experiments on twins and when they gave birth they used the babies. Those forty women were to disappear. As soon as the Russians were coming, the Germans started to sort them out, because they were witnesses to all that. Most were caught, but others managed to hide in the roofs and some escaped in the end. The Germans were hunting all these, so our *appels* in the morning were terrible because they never found the count right.

The other Polish woman helped me by getting me work on the *gartenkolonne*, in the SS garden. But it was full winter, there was nothing to do, so we hid down in a trench and we passed the time by her teaching me a few words of Polish. I taught her a few words of English. She was suspected of political activity – no trial or anything, she was only suspected – and one day, the SS came to fetch her. Other Poles told me that she was raped and hung in the chimney of the crematorium.'

The evacuation of the camp began at the end of February. We dared not go out in the streets of the camp for groups of women were often pounced upon by the offizieren to be sent immediately on transport, and these were often the 'black transports'. The blocks were emptied one after the other. The big tent in the centre of the camp was broken down; there were one or two skeletons found under the beds. The food became rarer, the soup sometimes only arriving at night. One day, the 1st March, everybody was ordered out, so in a few minutes we were outside with all our worldly possessions in a linen bag. We left Ravensbrück, a long column of 3,000 women marching five abreast. We each received a loaf of bread and a small packet of margarine and sausage as food for the journey, which was reckoned to last four or five days. We waited two hours until we were cold to the bone before the train arrived. Then we were pushed into cattle trucks – 70 or more women to a truck.

Precise details are by now insignificant for our purposes but a study by Francine Plisnier-Ladame, using the camp records kept to the end by the fanatically accurate S.S. bureaucracy, reports that the big transport left for Mauthausen on 7th March. It included 1247 'politicals' of whom 291 were Belgians.

Mauthausen

The Mauthausen concentration camp near Linz had been founded as a business enterprise by the SS in 1938, after the *Anschluss* with Austria, with a quarry as its profit-making core. In 1941 it was classified by Heydrich as the harshest of all camps, for men judged as inveterate enemies of the Reich, in a grade on its own even above that of those in the top rank of severity – Dachau, Buchenwald and

Sachsenhausen. It was not designed for quick, mass exterminations, but to wear out prisoners by exceptionally hard labour and low diet so that they would never emerge. It became the centre of a cluster of satellite camps. Executions by shooting were regular, and it had a gas chamber and crematorium at the castle of Hartheim, about twenty miles away, which was used, at first, mainly to dispose of handicapped people. By 1945, this took prisoners too sick or weak to work. From 1942, Mauthausen had its own gas chamber and had a section for Russians, who were not used for work but simply starved to death. During late 1944 and early 1945, its organisation was overwhelmed by thousands of prisoners from camps such as Auschwitz, evacuated to avoid their liberation by the Russian advance.

This is Elsie's story of her six weeks there.

Then followed the most painful journey of all. It started snowing and freezing once more. We journeyed south, crossing Czechoslovakia to Mauthausen in Austria, one of the worst reputed camps for men. In each truck was an SS and an offizierin who had the luxury of straw to sleep on; there were also two tin pails for lavatory use. The first day we were able to get water to drink, but the following days we only had snow to quench our thirst. As for washing, that was out of the question. The truck E. and I were in had been used for transporting coal, so after four days and four nights in that truck the result can be imagined. We had no covers and no exercise. All day long the truck was open and the cold was bitter. E's feet became frozen and she suffered badly from this.

At last after nearly five days we arrived at Mauthausen on the Danube, not far from Linz. It was night and the village was quite picturesque under the snow, but the camp was built on a height and it was a five mile walk. The column, always five abreast, started the climb, but after such a journey many women could hardly walk. Those who fell behind were put on the side of the road, and a few seconds later a rifle shot told us that their sufferings were ended for ever. E. advanced with great difficulty with her frozen feet and I passed the most anxious moments trying to help her along. It is marvellous what an encouragement to advance those rifle shots were, however, and at last we reached the top and entered the camp. It was still snowing and we were glad of the mug of hot coffee received in the open. We waited all night long, standing in the open until the next midday before it was our turn. All our clothes were taken to be disinfected, and one by one we were examined for vermin. All those working at the baths were men. We were the first large convoy of women to be lodged at the camp. We were placed one by one on a stool with our arms raised. One man searched with the end of a pencil for lice whilst another brushed us with disinfectant, those with lice being shaved altogether. After the shower-bath we were obliged to pass in the streets of the camp in the wind to arrive at our block.

Here we had no beds. Straw sacks were placed close to each other on the floors of the barracks, and four women allotted to each straw sack. Even packed together like this there was not room for everyone. The nights were terrible; we awoke (if we had the luck to be able to sleep) stiff and more tired than ever. The Commandant of the camp had thought first of sending us on further but finally it was decided to find work for us in the camp. There had been a spirit of revolt just before our arrival and our presence there created a diversion for the men. Accordingly there were women sent to work in the laundry, in the offices, in the sewing rooms etc. It was necessary to be young (even for the sewing no one over 40 was accepted) and able to support a little joke or two. All those chosen for these jobs were given quite smart little dresses and jackets and received more food. One day the Commandant came to sort out the remaining women. He examined each woman in turn to see if she was not too old or thin or too weak in the legs. All the weak ones were sent to another block and a little while later sent for transport.

The weather changed for the better and we were happy to be able to spend the best part of the day sitting or lying on the ground outside in the yard. One of our chief occupations was searching for lice in each other's hair. We watched the arrival of the bread and pounced on the crumbs that fell on the ground. The Blokova, a German with short cut hair and dressed in shirt blouse and trousers, was continually smoking cigarettes and amusing herself with those who did the service for food etc. These women received food and visits from the men. They were constantly cooking potatoes, meat, eggs pancakes, and so on, on the fire. We others had the benefit of the smell. The food question became more and more acute. We tried to get work for the sake of the extra soup.

Young Elsie adds one episode her Mother chose not to tell. At Amstetten, twenty miles east of Mauthausen, the railway station had been bombed by American aircraft, and women prisoners including the Elsies were taken to a satellite camp there to help clear the tangled wreckage. 'Once, we were machine-gunned by an aircraft and all started running to some trees. Mummy was not strong and stumbled but we helped her up and got to cover. We were working all the time, with spotlights on at night. I had a dreadful cold. As I had nothing to sneeze in I found a piece of material to use. It made a bump in my pocket and when work finished, we had to put ourselves five by five to be searched to see if we had stolen anything. I had this bump and they ordered me to go to the top of the pile of wreckage, stand there and they said, "Undress!" They made me undress on top there in the freezing cold.

Then, suddenly, a French girl had a sort of hysteria crisis, screaming, and they all pounced on her to keep her quiet and didn't look at me, so very quickly I put my clothes on again and slowly got down, put my scarf over my head and made myself very, very small. So I escaped what had happened to another woman they had caught: they put her in the middle of the camp and made all the other prisoners go round and sing German songs while they kicked her to death.'

After a few days, the women were all so weak that they could do no useful work on the wreckage and stayed at Mauthausen. Ten Belgians were among thirty-four women prisoners killed during the Allied raid and others died of wounds.

We resume Elsie's story.

The average death rate was about 200 a day. The crematorium was continually in use and our 'blok' being not far off, we continually had this horrible odour in our noses. The walls of the camp were in blocks of granite and iron rings were built in the walls at regular intervals. Men were chained to these rings as punishment, and beaten or left there until they died. From outside the camp there was a stone stairway of 186 steps leading down to a quarry. The walls of the camp had been built by prisoners who had had to bring the blocks of granite up from the quarry and if this was not done to the taste of the SS the men were forced to throw themselves from the top into the quarry.

Prisoners evacuated from other camps were arriving in Mauthausen, and food was becoming scarcer. A column of 1,200 women was removed from the camp to the quarry below and lodged in a former munition factory. E. and I were amongst these. We were more crowded than ever. The only water for all purposes was a small stream that ran close to the building. The dandelions that grew near were soon uprooted by the prisoners. Our comrades who worked in the potato column brought us a few raw potatoes from time to time, which probably saved our lives at this moment. For a week or more we were fed on soup made from the lights and tripes of exhausted horses coming from the front. Then started a period of beetroot soup and the bread was reduced to a small slice a day, very often quite green and mouldy. The sanitary conditions became worse and worse. The WCs consisted of four large wooden receptacles (with a plank placed across) at the exterior of the building. After a few hours these were overflowing on to the ground, making an awful mud that finally found its way into our little stream. From that moment we licked our bowls clean rather than wash them in the stream. To get to the w.c. at night was a supplice for every square inch of ground was occupied by sleepers and one had to climb over them in the dark. To tread on someone's legs or body was liable to finish in a fight. It became more and more a struggle for life. At one end of the building a few beds were put up for the ill and some of the prisoners devoted themselves to looking after these.

One memorable moment we had was when all the Norwegians were called for, and the rumour had it that they were going to a Red Cross camp. Hope sprang high again for a few days, and we heard that the Russians were only 60 kilometres away. Days and weeks passed again. We became so weak and weary and apathetic that it became more and more necessary to shout at us and beat us to make us move. One morning I woke up feeling very ill and hardly knew what was going on around me. In the evening I was put into a bed with 40 degrees Centigrade of fever.

Young Elsie adds: 'She had pneumonia and all day long I was going to fight to try to get her a bed, because she was sleeping on the ground near me. There were a few beds left for the ill people and finally, in the evening, I got someone to help to take her there. There were no drugs. I brought her some water and then I went to negotiate with the Gypsies to buy her two sugar lumps, giving our food ration in exchange.* Five days later, she still had a very high temperature, but I told her that we would soon see Bob. I had heard an old Wehrmacht soldier (there were no young ones left) say, *"Bald nach Hause* [home soon]!"'

---

* The Gypsies and other groups such as Spanish Republicans had by now set up a corruption system. The lump sugar was from Red Cross parcels stolen by the camp management.

LIBERATION

Young Elsie was not simply trying to raise her mother's spirits. The SS and prisoners alike all knew that the Third Reich was in its last days and streams of prisoners from outlying camps to the east were being herded along the valley below, dying in hundreds as they marched. But what would the SS do with the red triangle 'politicals'?

I remained three or four days in bed, always with fever, and was still there when the order came for all French and Belgians to return to the camp. The ill ones went in a lorry and the others climbed the 186 steps. We spent the night in a 'blok' and the next morning were marched, still five abreast, out of the camp and were left waiting on a flat stretch of ground on the side of the hill. Where were we going? And how? Could it be true that we were going to a Red Cross camp? But no – that was too beautiful a dream. Were we going on cattle trucks like the last time or in the black transport?

Her daughter's version is: 'I went up the 186 steps with the others and we were shut in the showers inside the camp. At night, the Camp Commandant hesitated whether to gas us; we were in the right building for it. He was negotiating with the Red Cross.* Then in the morning we were taken through the gate in a column, five by five, to a flat place near an immense excavation; the crematoriums weren't quick enough so they made big holes and put the corpses in them, covered with lime.'

This is how Elsie ends her war story.

Then someone saw, climbing the hill, a white lorry with a huge red cross on it – then others – a long column of them coming in our direction. We could hardly believe our eyes. Then at last we realised that it was really true, this story of the Red Cross taking us over. Tears came into our eyes and we could not speak for emotion.

---

* Ziereis, the SS officer who had run the camp since 1939, had earlier given orders that not a single prisoner should fall into Allied hands. He refused to let the Swiss Red Cross inside the camp for several days after the Elsies' convoy left and despite the presence of a Swiss Red Cross delegation kept the gas chamber going until fuel ran out and he blew up the apparatus.

One by one these wonderful lorries arrived close to us and there came down from them such splendid fellows. Each prisoner was given a lovely new blanket and a seat in a lorry. The Commandant arrived, but did not look so arrogant now, especially when the bread that was to be dealt out to us was refused by the Red Cross officers as being too mouldy. He was forced to order the bread of the SS to be brought down to us. It was the International Red Cross of Geneva that had arrived to effectuate an exchange of prisoners. It appears that they'd been working a year for that before being successful.

We were driven thro' Austria and Germany also without stopping. The end of the second day we arrived near the Swiss frontier. The battle for Konstanz was in full swing and columns of retreating German troops passed us. It was only the next morning at 8 a.m. as we actually crossed the Swiss frontier that we really dared to breathe freely and to feel that we were out of the reach of the SS What a difference when the kindly Swiss people asked us to come this way, instead of shouting and the blows to which we had become accustomed.

The day before, in Germany, it had been dull weather and even some snow had fallen, but our first day in Switzerland the sun was shining in a clear blue sky, the grass was so green and the fruit trees all in blossom — a very symbol of stepping out of prison into a land of kindness and peace and liberty.

The two Elsies' very survival had been inseparably intertwined. Her daughter's account of their liberation is this. 'We went as quickly as possible, through everything. Sometimes we were stopped by officers, but we took no notice. One man spread his arms to stop us, but we didn't. After the first day, we stopped in a small camp at Ravensburg. [North of the Bodensee – Lake Constance.] Mummy's temperature went up again and I got her some medicines and a place in a lorry where she could lie down for the next day. When we arrived on the border, at a high point with a sort of no man's land down the slope, there were 'phone calls. The Germans didn't want to let us go; we were ordered to get out of the lorries and there were orders to shoot us. The 'phone calls and talking went on a long time and then the Red Cross told us, "Get back into the lorries slowly, very slowly." When one lorry was full, it went downhill without any engine noise to the border and others followed before the Germans noticed and then shots were fired, killing some prisoners.

In Austria and Germany the weather was grey but in Switzerland the sun was shining. There was liberty, civility; perfect – from captivity to peace. We were taken to a school in St Gall where we were moved to tears by the kindness of the nurses who came to hold us – no more screaming, no more knocks. They washed us, brushed our hair, disinfected us, took off the lice, and we let ourselves be treated like babies. When Mummy had been cared for, we went to sleep on nice, fresh straw in one of the classrooms. We received only very small quantities at a time to eat, our stomachs being retracted. Then we could send a telegram to the family to tell them that our return was near. Ill as she was, Mummy wanted to go back in the quickest possible way to see my brother and we only stayed three days. Others, including Yvette Guilmin, were so ill that they remained in hospital; some died there.

In France, we went to Lyons and travelled by slow train going north to Mons, along with other liberated French and Belgians.* We were about the first survivors of the camps to get into the country and at each little station the train stopped, the local band played the *Marseillaise* and the people willingly gave us soup, wine, milk, bread, cakes. We had too much! In Mons, I remember that in the train I was as sick as anything through overeating! To me, it was a treasure to see bread. We got those long French baguettes and I kept them; I didn't want to lose them, they were so precious! When I got back to Brussels, my grandmother saw me holding one and said "What's that? Now let's throw that away." I was furious! I was so cross with her! To me that bread was a priceless treasure!

At Mons, Belgian representatives of the Red Cross wanted to make us wait for instructions and identification papers, but we would not hear of that and many of us took the next train to Brussels where on 1st May at the Gare du Midi we were met with tears of joy by Bob, Grandmother, Auntie Esther, her son Paul and Uncle Marcel. Major Ford [the British Director of the Allies' Brussels office set up to find and assist those who had helped evaders] was there and after a superficial medical examination we were free to go 'home' which was to be at Grandmother's place.

---

* They were at some point issued with documents from a Belgian Commissariat for Repatriation office in Annecy.

The story finishes here and a new life had come. We were to speak very little of our adventures because we only encountered incomprehension and it disturbed some people. But I shall never forget nor forgive the Final Solution – the systematic extermination of entire transports of prisoners – Jews, Gypsies, Russians and others of many different kinds. To do so would be making cheap the life of every victim.'

Elsie soon after her return to Brussels

AND THEN …

After the welcomes at the station, the Elsies' new life began with very obvious handicaps in a city which had been getting on with its own business for eight months since liberation. They arrived in their Ravensbrück jackets, still smelling of the crematorium smoke, penniless, homeless and ill. Major Ford met the cash problem with a substantial grant. Their quick return had taken Grandmother by surprise, just as she was about to move to a smaller apartment, but she took them home with her and put them to bed.

Liberated journalists' business led them to push into the house wanting stories and photographs and, when firmly refused both, they had their revenge by suggesting that beneath the bedclothes, the ladies' shapes were no longer feminine. Their emaciated state was indeed Robert's first impression; he remembers that their upper arms were thinner than their forearms because they had one bone rather than two and that they each weighed little over 30 kilos (just over five stone). Their first quick medical check had found Elsie with symptoms of pulmonary TB, arteriosclerosis, hypertension and scabies; it predicted 50 per cent disability and for Young Elsie, 15 per cent disability.

At least Elsie was well provided with friends and on that first day, M. and Mme Hunez were welcome visitors. They discovered Grandmother's impending move and for the following day, in Young Elsie's words, 'They invited us to stay in their luxurious apartment. We soaked with delight in a warm, perfumed bath, then sank with utter bliss in those marvellous soft beds. After a while, I found I couldn't sleep, being too warm and comfortable, so I got out of bed and slept on the floor. These kind people found some clothes for us (the shops were empty) and we received some fine linen. What luxury! We were beautifully pampered, fed and fussed about – and how we enjoyed it!'

They then returned to live with Grandmother in her new apartment. She, too, had her own hard time during the war years, losing her eldest son, fighting to secure Robert's release, and then caring for the unhappy boy as well as her dying husband in the miserable conditions of the occupation. Now, in her tough Flemish farming style she accepted Elsie and her children for the next two years. Elsie had a bed in Grandmother's bedroom and Young Elsie and Robert slept in attics.

Robert had been spared the camps but since he saw his mother and sister disappear into *Nacht und Nebel* his teenage years, still on the GFP's list of suspects, had been traumatic enough. He first heard of his father's execution from a newspaper at his aunt's house. He then tried to protect his Grandparents by not speaking of it and found that they were doing the same for him. His Grandfather survived, suffering, until just after Brussels was liberated. Soon after that, Robert had to attend the ceremony of the reburial in the Enclos des Fusillés of his father and others shot at the Tir National. The photograph shows him standing, downcast, alongside his Uncle Marcel (by then in uniform), who had spared him the task of identifying the exhumed remains. It is understandable that despite the sympathy of the patriots among his teachers, he could not settle to school work as his parents had urged.

The Reburial (Robert, second from right, with his uncle)

With his mother and sister back, the cloud lifted dramatically. By the end of June, he startled his teachers by rising from twentieth to fifth in his class and so qualified to enter the national Faculty of Agronomy Sciences at Gembloux in the Autumn. Young Elsie quickly decided that at 21, instead of taking up her place on the

111

three-year nursing course at the Institut Edith Cavell, she should start earning her own living as soon as possible, so she went to stay with her godmother to prepare for the entrance examination in early September for two-year training as a physiotherapist.

Elsie herself had not come back for sympathy or convalescence, but to find work to provide for the children during their higher education. Her campaign began with a few weeks' work in a British Forces Club where she made a lasting friendship with an English WVS worker. She gave English lessons, one pupil being the son of a former fellow cell-mate, and took typing lessons from 'Constance' Liègeois. Although late in July another medical examination found her health hardly improved, she found temporary clerical work and finally in October, after a short visit to her family and a few of her English friends (being given 'a useful little sum' by her College year group), she became an invoicing clerk for an agricultural machinery firm, an uncongenial job she held for the next five years. Already Young Elsie was hard at work on her Physiotherapy course and Robert had written when she was in England assuring her with new confidence that he could handle his start at Gembloux, coming 'home' only at weekends.

Elsie and children, Brussels 1945

She had quickly discovered that the war could not be left behind. A week after the Elsies' group arrived back in Brussels, the brother-in-law of Mme Chaudoir, one of thousands of relatives of NN prisoners who never came back, wrote asking for news and describing her as tall, energetic and well-built. Elsie answered by return post that she had been sent from Ravensbrück to the Camp de Jeunesse. He politely wrote back his thanks. A month later came an invitation to one of many memorial masses for those who had disappeared with no funeral. Georges' third memorial mass was on their wedding anniversary, the 21st June, and later came the first annual memorial mass for the 150 members of Comet who had died – always on the Sunday nearest 20th October, the date of his execution along with the other eight of the line's first casualties.

By the same post as the Chaudoir inquiry had come a letter from the Inspector-General of Georges' Ministry, apologising for having only just heard of the Elsies' return and declaring that the ministry was honoured to have had Georges, 'the great patriot and soldier' in its ranks. He concluded with the offer of any help in his power as the family picked itself up and Elsie probably used this as she, shrewdly if unwillingly, set about acquiring documentation of the family's war record, vital in bureaucratic Belgium. Within a month, she had certification from the head of the Sureté evasion service that the Elsies had been condemned to death and become political prisoners in his service; a month later after going to the Sureté herself, she obtained a formal statement that Georges had been killed in its service. This was only a first move in a process which would drag on for the next three years.

The most prompt and practical help came from Major Ford and his American colleague in the Allied unit set up to trace Resistance survivors. In June came a second instalment of the grant Ford gave on 1st May and in September they both signed a carefully expressed letter, inviting Elsie to accept another larger sum equal to that due to the widow of an Allied soldier killed in action, although they recognised that 'the blood of a hero "ne se paye pas" [is not repayable].' In December, three-quarters of Young Elsie's study fees were awarded by the Belgian Ministry of Defence but then for three years it was up to Elsie to manage as best she could.

Successful RAF evaders had met in Paris before the war ended and obtained Air Ministry support for the RAF Escaping Society, aiming to trace and help the helpers who had suffered on their behalf. Some of them met and fêted Dédée soon after she returned from Mauthausen and many individuals – Bob Frost was one – returned to visit their hosts as soon as they could take leave. The Comet memorial mass became the focus of an *amicale* including escapers which soon turned the events into weekend reunions. At first, the RAF flew the escapers across but when this ended, wives came too and, now with second generation members, formal reunions continued until 2001. Elsie was one of those who did not wish to look back; that weekend was too painful an anniversary. Some of her 'boys' however traced her. In March, 1946, the first of them, Ivan Davies, addressed a letter to 'Resistance Movement, Brussels', asking to be put in touch with Monsieur Maréchal whose wife had been Elsie Bell and 'had a daughter now about nineteen years and a son about seventeen.' A month later it found its way to Elsie via the US Forces Brussels HQ. She replied, establishing a long-distance friendship which included Ivan's wife. In 1968 Ivan returned to thank his helpers and, after he and Elsie died, his wife and Young Elsie kept in touch. Ralph Van Den Bock corresponded with Elsie and came to attend the memorial mass for Mme Davreux in Namur with Madeleine Davreux and Young Elsie who had carried her body in Ravensbrück.

Earl Price was in touch for the rest of Elsie's life and in 1974 persuaded Young Elsie to travel from Burundi to join a Comet party's visit to Canada and the USA. During this, he took her to his home and insisted that he and his wife must vacate their bedroom for her, as she had left hers for him thirty-two years earlier.

Elsie kept the letters and enjoyed the friendship but nostalgia was not for her and she had present work to do. By October, 1947, she had paid for a new small flat with just enough room for three, Young Elsie had gained her Diploma with distinction and started work in the practice of one of her professors. Robert had distinctions in his second year examinations having earned what he could by working during vacations in the Institute's experimental gardens. His mother had meanwhile taken the precaution of obtaining a Sureté letter certifying that he, too had been imprisoned in its service; it added, for good measure, that the whole family's service was 'amongst the most effective in the struggle against the oppressor.'

Somehow, during 1946, Elsie had also found time and energy to illustrate a book of *Poems and Songs of Prisoners* written by Yvette Guilmin, the fellow prisoner and member of the line who worked for Greindl after the family's arrest. In addition to one drawing of Young Elsie smuggled out of St Gilles, she created a simple style for a series of cartoons illustrating prison life to punctuate a parody of a popular song. They convey better than words her capacity to see humour in bad times, but both poems and cartoons end at Waldheim. Ravensbrück and Mauthausen were beyond mockery.

Warm contacts with England were being kept up. Her brother, Stanley, and his wife came to Brussels; Young Elsie and Robert went to England together. In the summer of 1948, both Elsies visited London and Gorleston but there was a setback that Autumn when Young Elsie developed pleurisy and had to spend some months recovering in the clear air of Switzerland, fortunately with a grant from the Belgian organisation for war orphans.

By then, in one of the odder consequences of the war, Belgian officialdom had at last reduced to the dimensions of its filing cabinets the spontaneous heroism of unarmed Resistance members such as that of the Maréchals. Using a legal fiction first devised in the safe leisure of exile in London in 1942 to cover them against possible legal action after the war for acts against people or property, they would be retrospectively enlisted as agents of a Service of Information and Action which was not actually set up by law until February 1946. Then members of the already disbanded Service were enrolled by a committee of leaders of the different unarmed resistance groups, including Dédée, who had sent out her own enquiry forms to Comet members in the previous October. Mme Hassé, too, had in January sent the Sureté a detailed statement on Georges' work in *Luc* and in *Les Trois Mousquetaires*, with a copy to Elsie. As in all occupied countries, people who had done little or nothing, and even collaborators trying to cover their tracks, claimed to have been resisters and it was 1948 before 60 per cent of the applications had been rejected and enrolment was completed. This was not all. Each of the 18,716 enrolled was allotted a rank, but by an excess of bureaucratic refinement an individual's rank was only for his or her share on specified dates of action.* This mountainous

* Late in 1948, Georges was posthumously allotted the rank of Lieutenant from the date of his arrest and late in 1950 those of Auxiliary 2nd Class from June 1941 and 1st Class from January 1942. In May 1951, Young Elsie was ranked Auxiliary 1st class from 1st August 1942 and Adjutant (her father's World War rank) from 17th November 1942 to 1st May, 1945. At the same time, Elsie was ranked Auxiliary 1st Class, beginning particularly oddly from 1st November 1942, amended in October to 1st August 1942.

labour produced nothing useful for the Elsies, though it provided a basis for the equally tardy award of Belgian war decorations.

More practically useful, though almost as slow, was the work of the Association of the Condemned to Death, founded immediately after their liberation from Dachau by a group of Comet members, led by Jean-François Nothomb, 'Franco', who had taken over when Dédée was arrested. This led to the creation of an official roll of political prisoners in 1948. Urged by Mme Warnon, Elsie applied for enrolment and after attestations by her companions in prison, her acceptance in July 1948 yielded helpful, if not generous, quarterly grants as well as other minor benefits such as half price railway tickets.

Medals are often more sceptically viewed by warriors than by onlookers, but after wars there is a genuine wish to honour unselfish courage. In this matter, Britain and the USA also forestalled Belgium, being less beset by the problems of a government returning from four years' exile. They each began with certificates for identified helpers of their servicemen, the American over General Eisenhower's printed signature and the British by that of Air Marshal Tedder. The Air Ministry had pompously insisted on this because the RAF had principally benefited, though Churchill had offered to sign each one personally. Next came more formal, embossed diplomas, that from the US President presented at a public ceremony and that of the British Prime Minister, Attlee, sent merely by post. Georges' copy came in May 1946; the Elsies' a year and a half later.

The Americans produced a special award, the Medal of Freedom, for Resistance members. These were presented in Brussels at a lavish investiture in February 1947, perhaps because the US was then involved in Belgian politics, backing those who were refusing to let King Leopold return to rule; Hitler had deported him to Germany when the Allies landed in Normandy.

The British award was stylish but more modest and came later, in June 1948 when Comet members including the Elsies received from the British Ambassador at a ceremony in the Great Hall of the Palais des Beaux Arts a commendation for brave conduct and a small emblem similar to that of a Mention in Despatches for the British forces. However, Comet's special work for the RAF had been marked very early by the investiture of Dédée with the George Medal by King George in person, the first award to any one other than a Briton, even more strikingly followed by its award also to 'Michou' Dumon who took over after the betrayal of 'Franco' and Mme De Greef, from whose house near Bayonne every crossing of the Pyrenees was run. 'Nadine' Dumon received the OBE. Elvire Morelle, Peggy Van Lier and the D'Oultremonts each received an MBE.

The leader of another major escape line, Dr Albert-Marie Guérisse, a Belgian Army medical officer, received the George Cross rather than the George Medal because he had been given the protection of combatant status as 'Lieutenant-Commander Patrick O'Leary' of the Royal Navy. Foot and Langley comment that 'more or less equal services were unequally rewarded: an instance of the intricacies of the British system, which not even the British altogether understand.'

For the Maréchals, the first major Belgian act of public recognition was in October 1947 when a plaque was unveiled in the Ministry of Economic Affairs, commemorating its eight members who had died for the country. Each was the subject of a formal eulogy from the Secretary-General.* Eventually, in February 1948, Belgian medals began to arrive with Georges' posthumous award of the Order of Leopold with Palm, a higher order than that of Leopold II which he had received in 1930, along with the Croix de Guerre with Palm, Resistance Medal and Commemorative War Medal with two Stars. In the following month, each of the Elsies received the Knight's Cross of the Order of Leopold II, the Croix de Guerre with Palm, the Resistance Medal and the Croix du Prisonnier Politique and as late as January 1951, Elsie was invited to yet another ceremony to receive Georges' Croix du Prisonnier Politique with four Stars. Georges' recognition was important for the family but they set little store by their own honours – so much so that their English family only heard of them from Robert after Elsie's death. As Young Elsie puts it, 'For us, the medals were superficial. We did it and that was all.' Nearly fifty years later every one of these medals was stolen from 'Young' Elsie's safe.

Far more important on Elsie's scale of values was the achievement of her aims for her children. Soon after Young Elsie's return from Switzerland, in April 1949, she married and moved into her own home in Brussels where her mother became a regular weekend visitor. In October 1950 Robert and his mother spent five

---

* See Appendix I

117

days with their English family after he had completed with high honours his distinctive Gembloux course of *Ingénieur* in applied agronomy, the nearest English equivalent being a Master's degree. He had also at the Institut met Marie-Louise, an assistant there; they married in December and in the New Year set off for a research station in the Congo, where Robert began his life's work, specialising in applied genetics, initially of cotton and later of food legumes.

Elsie's five years of hard work in a job which could hardly have suited her tastes and talents less had succeeded and sealed the love – amounting to reverence – with which Elsie and Robert still speak of their mother. 'She did it by sheer love and will power.' Now she had seen them through to adult freedom and was herself free to give up account clerking and choose her own way of life.

Young Elsie and Robert after the war

FREEDOM

Although she was half-disabled, for Elsie vegetating was never an option. With just enough to live on in a very modest way, she made her later years an opportunity to strengthen family ties, develop old and new friendships, read new books, travel, explore new ideas and at last have more time for drawing and painting.

Visiting family and old friends in England, she felt that some of them looked and behaved as if the last twenty eventful years had left them deplorably unchanged. She brought her unmarried younger sister Olive to Brussels for a new outfit and hairstyle (her bun removed) at the hands of Elsie's hairdresser, who had become another friend. A much later photograph of the trio has them posed symbolically at the Atomium, built for the 1958 World Exhibition and still the greatest modern monument in Brussels.

Olive   Hairdresser   Elsie
Atomium created for 1958 Brussels Expo

Her friendship with 'Nounou' Warnon and 'Constance' Liègeois, forged in the camps, was particularly important to Elsie, who was attracted by their footloose way of life. After the war they unsuccessfully tried various types of farming and then moved back to Brussels, where Constance took temporary office jobs if funds ran short as they pursued new enthusiasms – amateur painting in dashing style and, most of all for Nounou, Theosophy and Eastern Religions. They remembered Elsie's courage and sense of humour in their hardest times and admired her constantly questioning mind; Constance says, *'Polly était toujours étudiante!'* Elsie was open-minded but never swept away by their passions. Although, for instance, they urged her to paint in their style she experimented with looser brushwork but still with the disciplines of her trained eye and hand and she changed her use of colour only in response to new experience.

Robert and Young Elsie who in 1954 also emigrated to the Congo were the agents of this. On Robert's first home leave in that year, after staying in her flat with his wife and first son, he took them all to Villefranche on the Côte d'Azur, where the Mediterranean light and colour came as a revelation to Elsie. This and the effect on her health led her to winter there away from the smoke and chill of Brussels as often as possible. Even more exciting was the impact of visits to Africa in 1956 and 1958, the second lasting several months and taking her from Congo to the green mountains of Burundi, where Young Elsie now lived, and where she learned a little Swahili to help her meet African people and children. Elsie's reaction to tropical sunshine and the flowers which Robert loved to name was a flood of brilliantly coloured paintings which still fill his house walls.

An old pocket diary which she used as a private notebook for several years offers insights into her thinking. It contains not only Swahili vocabulary but a very varied reading list ranging from birdlife and popular science to poems, novels and eastern religions. Simone de Beauvoir's *La Force des Choses* published in 1963, when Elsie entered her seventieth year, suggests curiosity about the existentialists. She also used the diary as she wrote poems and verses, some short and lighthearted and others personal reflections. The longest ponders her search to answer her question 'From where do we come and to where do we go?' 'I've searched in vain ... As each veil is lifted the mystery thickens.' It ends, after repeating the question, 'Serene and content, I reply "I don't know."' This cannot be dated but its refusal to accept the conclusions others offered may well relate to Nounou's decision in 1960 to go to India, where she spent some years in an ashram.

Elsie with grandson Georges in the Congo

In 1958 Elsie had rented a house to share with Robert and his family for his home leave and Nounou suggested that, rather than return to her flat for the few months left before she set off on her second African journey, she should sell it and move in with her and Constance. She agreed and during the removal, Constance persuaded her to take the major emotional step of disposing of Lilian's clothes and toys. On her return, she took a smaller flat into which, when Nounou went to India in 1960, Constance moved, to devote the next nine years to helping Elsie as she fought to remain active despite growing ill-heath and disability, now rated at 60 per cent.

1960 was a landmark year for her in another way. Congo's independence from Belgian rule in July was followed by an Army mutiny and the breakup of the state, which forced Robert to bring back his family as a precaution. Three years of adventure and abortive attempts to resume his work and family life in the Congo culminated in robbery by Ethiopian UN soldiers of everything except the clothes he, his wife and three children were wearing, so from 1963, Gembloux became his permanent home, only 30 miles from his mother. Now she could see more of her grandchildren, and Jean recalls that it was she who introduced them to Walt Disney. Robert, with his precious genetic samples saved, became a Professsor in the Institute, strongly linked with fellow-researchers in Britain and elsewhere. When in 1962 Burundi also became disturbed, Young Elsie returned to set up a practice in Brussels and was able to help her mother with exercises and advice as arthritis made walking increasingly difficult for her at a time before hip replacement was available.

Elsie in the South of France

With African travel impossible, Elsie and Constance left for England in May 1961 with a small trailer caravan for an ambitious four month car tour. From Kent they drove by stages to West Devon, by Bath and Stratford-upon-Avon across to Gorleston and then to Nottinghamshire for a month near Elsie's closest school friend from Yarmouth, Lily Seaton. Finally, they stayed with Olive and then

Stanley. Apart from sights seen and people met, Constance's most vivid memory is of how the humble caravan rocked with their laughter, especially at its contrast with the palatial mobile homes parked around them. Within a few months, they were again on the road to spend winter on the Côte d'Azur. This became their custom, with Constance contributing earnings from temporary jobs in Brussels, where a Gowen cousin from the USA once came to stay with them. Unfortunately, Young Elsie had to return to Burundi in 1964, from where she anxiously sent advice as a stream of cheerful postcards charted her mother's continuing travels.

Elsie in her retirement

In 1965, a quick trip to England (which proved to be the last) was followed, after a stay on the Côte, by a tour in the Pyrenees to stay at Amélie-les-Bains and explore some remote mountain roads during December and January. The next winter began with treatment for Elsie and Constance's mother, Rosa, in thermal springs at the Provence Alps spa of Gréoux-les-Bains. Elsie sceptically reported to Young Elsie, 'We are busy with our cure. Two hours of bed rest followed by a two-hour siesta.' At St Raphaël they encountered snow and stormy seas which Elsie painted in a style quite unlike any other of her work. Back in Brussels, a deep wound was touched by a letter informing her that Georges' coffin had been again moved. His memorial cross remained in the Clos des Fusillés, but Schaerbeek had created a *Pelouse d'Honneur* for its war dead and there his remains now lie.

Later that year, Elsie suffered a heart attack which confined her to a wheelchair, so there was no winter travel, but by June 1968 she was in the small Belgian seaside town of Koksijde from where she sent her very worried daughter a picture postcard of children leaping on the beach. 'Booked our own apartment here for a month – 3rd storey but my chair goes easily in the lift. Rosa and I have already tried the Pale Ale – also a variety of wind, cold, rain and nice warm sunshine. The air is already doing us good, I believe. Rosa has difficulty in walking and I can't yet walk. It would be so much easier if I could run about like the youngsters on this card. I have taken note of your last list of exercises and clinics in Brussels.'

That Autumn she failed to have her disability rating raised; the examining doctor judged that her need for personal help arose from heart and arthritic problems which were constitutional rather than the result of her wartime experiences. She had to call off a last attempt at a Côte d'Azur winter when at Seillans, twenty miles from the sea, she conceded that she was too ill to continue.

Finally bedridden, on 27th February 1969, after a prominent former member of the Resistance visited her, the RAF Escaping Society representative in Brussels, Squadron Leader Edward Hearn, DFC asked her for a frank confidential statement of her needs. He suggested a consultation with Dr Guérisse, the famous 'O'Leary' who had also survived Mauthausen, and quickly followed up with a gift of money but on 25th March, still in her flat, nursed by Constance, she died. Young Elsie flew back from Burundi just too late to do more than help in arranging for her funeral to be conducted by the Church of England's chaplain in Brussels. Her grave is in the war memorial section of the Uccle communal cemetery, on the opposite side of the city from the Schaerbeek Pelouse d'Honneur.

Appendix 1

Allocution delivered by Secretary-General Baron Snoy et
d'Oppuers at the inauguration ceremony of a
commemorative plaque dedicated to eight officers
of the Department of Economic Affairs who died
for the mother-country during the war 1940–45.
Saturday, 18th October 1947

'Nos Seigneurs les Morts'

Each of the eight was the subject of an eulogy. The following is a
translation of the Secretary-General's words on Georges:

Georges Maréchal, shot at the Tir National on 20th October 1943,
entered the Administration on 27th November 1919 as an archivist
clerk at the Belgian High Commission at Coblence. He entered the
Ministry of Economic Affairs in 1932 and from 1935 carried out the
duties of inspector in the Administration of Internal Commerce.

An invalid of the 1914–1918 War, he had drawn from his
memories of the first war lessons of patriotism and activity in the
service of the allied armies which he could not forget and he devoted
himself to several espionage services in which his knowledge of
the German language was particularly valuable. His activity in the
lines collecting allied airmen, who with the co-operation of his wife
and daughter he guided and cared for with inexhaustible generosity,
earned him arrest on 18th November 1942 with all his family.
Submitted to repeated and cruel interrogations, Maréchal had the
courage to avoid any word, sign or act likely to compromise a
comrade. Condemned to death on 15th April, 1943, he was shot at
the Tir National and died in simple, brave heroism with a pride and
nobility which command admiration. His self-sacrifice and heroism
are a perpetual lesson for the Department.

POÈMES
ET CHANSONS
DES PRISONNIÈRES

D'YVETTE GUILMIN

Illustrations de POLLY MARECHAL

toutes deux condamnées à mort

___

Imprimerie Jacques GODENNE, s. a.
19-21, Rue de Bruxelles
Namur

1946

Sources

As is obvious, most of the text is based on private papers in the possession of Mme E. Maréchal and Professor R. Maréchal and on recorded conversations with them.

Information about Norwich Training College is based on archives of Keswick Hall College of Education held in the Norfolk County Record Office.

Printed sources used, mentioned or quoted in the text are listed below. Neave's are the only detailed accounts of Comet published in English. It would have been pretentious in a short memoir to add a full bibliography or to give references for statements about the context of the Maréchals' lives, but I shall be happy to answer postal inquiries addressed to me c/o the publisher.

W. E.

Baudhuin, E., *l'Economie Belge Sous l'Occupation 1940–1944*, 2nd edn, E. Bruyant, Brussels, 1945

Davies, I. H., *Rescued by Comet*, Privately published, Nedlands, W. Australia, n.d.

Foot, M. R. D., *Resistance*, Eyre Methuen, London, 1976

Foot, M. R. D. and Langley, J. M., *MI9: Escape and Evasion 1938–1945*, Bodley Head, 1970

Gillingham, J., *Belgian Business in the Nazi New Order*, Jan Dhondt Foundation, Ghent, 1977

Le Chêne, E., *Mauthausen: the history of a death camp*, Methuen, London, 1971

Lagrou, P., 'Perceptions alliés de la question royale' in M. Dumoulin et al., *Léopold III*, Editions Complexe, Brussels, 2001

Mommen, A., *The Belgian Economy in the Twentieth Century*, Routledge, London, 1994

Neave, A., *Little Cyclone*, Hodder and Stoughton, London, 1954

Neave, A., *Saturday at M.I.9*, Hodder and Stoughton, London, 1969

Plisnier-Ladame, F., *Les Femmes Belges dans les Camps Nazis*, Amicale des anciennes prisonnières politiques de Ravensbrück et Institut Emile Vandervelde, Brussels, 1990

Rémy, Réseau Comète. 3 vols., Librairie Acedémique Perrin, Paris, 1966, 1967, 1975

Strubbe, F., *Services Secrets Belges 1940–1945*, 3rd edn, Union des Services de Renseignements et d'Action, Madoc, Ghent, 2001

De Vasselot de Régné, O., *Tombés du Ciel: Histoire d'une Ligne d'Evasion*, privately published, Paris, 1999